Unexpected

A Memoir of Endurance
and Triumph in Raising
a Challenging Child

Maralee Parker

Life is hard.
Take it one day
at a time!
Matthew 6:34
Maralee
Parker

LITTLE CREEK PRESS
AND BOOK DESIGN
MINERAL POINT, WISCONSIN

Little Creek Press®
A Division of Kristin Mitchell Design, Inc.
5341 Sunny Ridge Road
Mineral Point, Wisconsin 53565

Book Design and Project Coordination:
Little Creek Press and Book Design

First Printing
March 2022

For more information or to order books,
www.littlecreekpress.com

Library of Congress Control Number: 2022903560

ISBN-13: 978-1-955656-16-0

Disclaimer: This book is a personal, descriptive story of what occurred
in our lives and is not meant to be prescriptive in any way for you. Please
consult your doctor or mental health worker with questions or concerns about
your specific situation. This story is true. Some names and places
have been changed for privacy reasons.

To Beth,
Who lives a challenging journey—one day at a time.
Thank you for giving permission to share it all:
The good, bad, and ugly to encourage
others along their way.

And to Greg,
My loving husband, who once was reluctant
but now is a champion for mental health
education and support.

Praise for *Unexpected*...

This story of Maralee's journey with her daughter, Beth, was insightful, gut-wrenching, and filled with faith and love. I want to thank her so much for putting herself out there to tell her story, as it will help others. I'm not as good at quoting Bible verses as she is, but my favorite is "I can do all things through Him who strengthens me" (Phil. 4:13). I could see that verse at work in Maralee and Greg's life every step of the way.

~Teri Latter, NAMI volunteer

Unexpected is a story of the mother's faith and endurance. Maralee's commitment and love for her daughter shine through as she gives readers a window into the intense daily challenges of parenting mental illness and Asperger's.

~Julie Hornok, author of the award-winning book
United in Autism, Finding Strength Inside the Spectrum

To any family navigating life with a loved one with mental health challenges, this book will give you the hope and support you need to push through another day. Maralee's words show others that they are not alone as she walks through her journey that not many can understand. This book is heartfelt, engaging and full of scripture-based encouragement.

~Nancy Binger, mom of a special-needs child

Unexpected is a tribute to faith, love, education, support and miracles. People who've parented children with special needs and/or mental illness will find themselves whispering "us, too," as they read through the Parkers' journey. 'Civilians' cannot know what it is like, so I am especially pleased that Maralee mentioned NAMI (National Alliance on Mental Illness). The free NAMI Family-to-Family course was a lifeline for my family, and the nonjudgmental welcome I received to NAMI Family Support groups was an emotional lifesaver. *Unexpected* is a gem.

~Laurie Huske, Immediate Past President,
NAMI Kane County North

As a social worker professor, counselor and a parent, I believe Maralee Parker's debut memoir, *Unexpected,* is one of the most important books to come along in years. This easy-to-read and very relatable book details the struggles Parker and her husband faced raising their adopted daughter Beth (now an adult), who experienced a range of difficult behavioral crises throughout her childhood. Parker details the challenges she faced as a mother who dearly wanted to love a child who seemed incapable of loving her back, challenges with other parents' well-meaning but often unhelpful and even shaming advice, and challenges to her faith life when prayer alone did not seem to be enough. Parker's readable and relatable memoir provides parents (and really anyone) with sage wisdom rooted in her Christian faith in a way that goes beyond common anecdotes and superficial answers. Parker provides struggling parents and family members with guidance in how to love a difficult child who may seem unlovable. But the lessons Parker provides extend beyond parenting and can be applied to any crisis that makes us question our faith in God and in ourselves. I plan on providing this book to every one of my clients who is struggling with family issues, particularly parenting challenges.

~Michelle Martin, PhD, MSW
Associate Professor of Social Work
California State University, Fullerton

Table of Contents

Introduction

Life didn't turn out the way I had expected. Does it ever? I had an agenda for a happy marriage (got that), two children (got that), a great career (got that), and a happy, peaceful life (that one was more challenging). Yet, looking back, my husband and I can trace the hand of God directing our lives through all the joys and challenges. He has His purposes. We've learned to trust Him, but it's an ongoing, daily goal to trust Him, not a once-and-done pledge.

"Why write a book?" you might ask. I want to encourage parents (or others) who have mentally ill loved ones to realize they are not alone. Living closely with someone with mental illness can be an isolating experience. There is no end in sight. Even when life gets hard—really hard—exhausted parents need to realize that many others are walking or have walked similar rough paths. It's brutal at times. Occasionally, there is a period of smooth sailing when families can catch their breath. Not in every case, but sometimes *there is recovery*. I love to attest that, in our case, this is true.

"Weeping may last through the night, but joy comes with the morning" (Psalms 30:5b). We are grateful our "morning" has arrived. We pray it stays. We love morning.

We want to encourage, support, and comfort all who are still in the trenches. We want them to know they are never alone. Many are walking a similar path—sometimes in secret because they are ashamed. Mental illness needs to be brought out into the open to erase the stigma associated with it. We must talk about it, seek help, and learn that many other families are experiencing similar struggles. With education, there will come understanding.

It's my prayer that this book will remind you that you're not alone. If you feel you are—and have no one to support you—reach out to your Heavenly Father, the source of all comfort. He sees all, knows all, and loves you more than you will ever comprehend.

All praise to God, the Father of our Lord Jesus Christ. God is our merciful Father and the source of all comfort. He comforts us in all our troubles so that we can comfort others. When they are troubled, we will be able to give them the same comfort God has given us.

2 Corinthians 1:3–4

1

Death Wish

" I hope you die."

Beth, my 12-year-old daughter, was obviously not very sympathetic as I headed off to the hospital for major surgery. The doctor was removing my left kidney and the cancer growing in and around it. I was 45 years old and not ready to leave this world.

My husband, Greg, and I had Beth, our challenging preteen, and her brother, Chad, who was 20. Chad was on his way out the door to an exciting, independent future. He was doing great. It was Beth I worried about as I faced this surgery. Not only did she have a typical, snarky teen attitude, but her brain was sick. We hadn't figured out exactly what was going on, but we knew Beth definitely had mental and emotional challenges. She was not normal. She was not emotionally able to handle the idea of losing her mom. We tried to keep the cancer details and worrisome possibilities under wraps around her; she had enough anxiety already. My big worry was, who would advocate for Beth if I didn't survive? She needed me, whether she would admit it or not.

She struggled with expressing appropriate emotion, but she excelled at showing anger and rage. Thus, her heartbreaking wish for me as I left the house for the hospital didn't destroy me. It made me sad, but I wasn't shocked. By this time, I knew her limitations and what to expect from her. I had learned to ignore much of what she said, letting it go in one ear and out the other. So much of it was impulsive ranting. Early on in this journey of raising Beth, I had accurately coined it "diarrhea of the mouth." Ugly stuff just came pouring out—often.

Of course, a "good parent" wouldn't let her child talk back. In the beginning, I tried to be that good parent. That was before I learned what I was facing with Beth. As the months and years went on, I realized I had bigger fish to fry. Beth's verbal abuse, nasty as it sometimes became, was not the war I chose to fight. There were other wars ahead that involved life and death.

Having kidney cancer in 2001 was a scary time in my life, as you might imagine. It all happened quickly, from seeing the first symptom to enduring multiple tests and having major surgery weeks later. I had vacillating emotions, from, *This can't be happening to me!* to *God, please don't let me die!* to *You are God, and I am not.* I would remind myself of Isaiah 55:9: "For just as the heavens are higher than the earth, so my ways are higher than your ways and my thoughts higher than your thoughts." *Help me trust You*, I prayed.

I had never felt greater love than during those weeks of uncertainty. Friends, coworkers, relatives, and church family all rallied around me. There were cards, texts, emails, visits filled with love and good wishes, and most importantly, promises of prayer. I heard from hundreds of people. Weirdly, it seemed like I was attending my own funeral—except I hadn't died—because of the outpouring of support. I felt the love.

I also had another happy incentive for getting past the surgery. Our son, Chad, was getting married in just eight weeks! As the groom's mother, I had to be there to be escorted down the aisle, enjoy the mother-son dance, and celebrate such a proud, happy, once-in-a-lifetime moment with him. I couldn't imagine not being there. I wouldn't imagine not being there.

The day of surgery came. The surgeon, who rated high on skill and low on bedside manner, did his job. I've always said I'll take skill over personality any day when choosing a surgeon. It wasn't an easy surgery to endure, nor was the recuperation fun. My left side was filled with hundreds of stitches, inside and out, and I was the proud owner of an 18-inch scar. But God heard the prayers of many, and the doctor was able to remove the kidney and adrenal gland and all of the cancer. It was a stage three cancer, but the arrogant but skilled doctor got it all. I was done. No chemo or radiation needed. I thanked God for answering our prayers.

Maralee Parker

When I returned home from the hospital, I found a piece of school notebook paper in Beth's backpack. Written in pencil, in large printed letters, was this message: "Welcome Home Mom." That made me very happy. It was the closest I would get to receiving affection from our daughter, even if I just *happened* to find it in her backpack. I don't think she would have given it to me.

Chad married his bride six weeks later, and this proud mama was there. It was a celebration of life, health, and great love.

And Beth didn't get her wish. I didn't die. ♥

2

Plan B

Let's go back to the beginning. It was 1983. My grand life plan indicated it was time to add to our family. Chad was born in 1980, and I felt three years between kids would be perfect. My premise was there'd be less chance of competition between them, yet they'd still be close enough in age to hang out together. I saw that competition play out firsthand all of my life with my two brothers, who are 17 months apart (seven and nine years older than me). I was convinced that three years between my children would be perfect.

So, let the trying-to-conceive games begin! They did, and we didn't. We tried to get pregnant for a year, and then fertility experts recommended that we visit a fertility doctor.

After our visit with the doctor, we boosted our chances of conception by taking fertility pills. They didn't help. After two or three years of this, we were done. That kind of stress is tough on a marriage. Month after month of repeated disappointment is hard to endure.

We decided to pursue adoption. We were very willing to love and raise someone else's baby—someone who, for whatever reason, couldn't take on that responsibility. We worked with an adoption agency, jumping through all the hoops. We became very proficient at jumping! That process took two-and-a-half years.

I remember one stressful night when the social worker visited us for the required home study. Of course, we were very nervous because I felt we had to be "perfect parents" to gain the agency's approval. Imagine my horror when our little dog peed on the carpet right in front of her.

Chad also accidentally spilled his drink while she was there. Lovely. There went our "perfect family" illusion.

She asked us questions, including, "Would you be willing to accept a special needs baby?" Greg and I knew that question would be asked. We had discussed it and felt we were not "called" to raise a child with special needs. In addition to parenting Chad, we were both career-minded, busy serving at church, and already had responsibilities with elderly family members. We didn't feel we had the emotional resources or time to invest in a child who would need special help. We wanted the perfect, healthy, cute newborn (preferably with a head full of hair). Was that too much to ask? We declined the special needs option but felt a little guilty doing so. The question made us feel as if we were at The Baby Store, picking exactly which model we wanted. We had already requested a girl—to go with our boy. Our perfect family would be complete with a sweet little girl—with no special needs, *thank you very much.*

Little did we know what was ahead, but God knew. It's best that we didn't know. God, in His wisdom, tells us to take life one day at a time and not worry about tomorrow. Each day, indeed, does have enough problems of its own.

God had a plan for Greg and me (just as He does for you), even though we weren't buying into it at first. We were trying to control our own destiny, but God gave us a detour named Bethany Brooke Parker. It's been a detour that has lasted for over 33 years now and will likely last until our dying day.

The agency we worked with allowed us to have a closed adoption. This meant there would be no contact with the birth parents while the child was still a minor. You might wonder why we chose that path. I had strong opinions about wanting it closed, and Greg agreed with me. I didn't want our child to be confused emotionally about who her parents were growing up. I didn't want her to have divided loyalty, especially during the sometimes turbulent teen years, when it would be very easy to say, "I'll just go live with my *real* mother!"

I knew that adoptees could already have identity, separation, and abandonment issues and felt that interacting with birth parents after the initial placement would not be beneficial.

So back to the home study. After it was concluded, we were told we had been approved. We were relieved to have passed the test! Then it became a matter of waiting.

The agency told us they would call when a baby became available. We were told to prepare by having the basics on hand (diapers, a few infant clothes, a crib) and wait for "the call." We tried to return to our normal routines, knowing that "the call" could come at any moment.

It took many, many months—more than a nine-month pregnancy. We received a letter about six months into the waiting time, encouraging us to be patient, promising they would let us know when a baby girl was available for us. Of course, the agency was working with other couples who also wanted to adopt. I learned years later that the agency would present several possible options to the pregnant woman or couple if both birth parents were involved. They let them choose the parents for their baby. It made me feel good to know that we were chosen to be Beth's parents, not just by God, but by the birth parents as well.

My friend, Sue, and I had fun preparing baby Bethany's nursery with fresh paint and cute wallpaper filled with pastel hues. I bought a crib and some baby necessities. Going to the infant department and buying all the cute baby things almost felt like a fantasy. I wondered, *Is this really going to happen? Am I pretend-pregnant?* I joyfully bought pink and purple girly outfits, blankets, and hair bows. I didn't know what season she would be arriving, so that was a bit tricky. I just wanted to be ready whenever that long-awaited call came. Chad was eight years old by this time, so we had long left the baby stage behind, with all of the helpful equipment (car seat, stroller, changing table, toys, highchair, playpen, swing, and more). We gathered items here and there, even at garage sales. We were excited to be nesting in preparation for the arrival of our new little pink bundle of joy.

And then we got the call. ♥

3

And Baby Makes Four

Writing and editing Christian education materials for kids was a fun and rewarding career. I loved my job, the mission, and the people I worked with each day. We were family and truly cared about each other. Each department was set up in one large area with portable walls, but there were no individual walls between editors, so there was little privacy for personal conversations. So, when my phone rang one morning in November 1988, the entire department soon became aware that I had finally received *the call!*

After almost three years of working with the adoption agency, the big day finally arrived. I was shaking with excitement. Our lives were about to change forever (oh, what an understatement). The agency said they had a little girl they'd like us to consider. She was 11 days old. "When could you come to meet her?" they asked.

"We can be there in an hour!" I enthusiastically responded. Then I called my husband with the big news. Though he is much more emotionally reserved than I, he was very excited as well. We met at home and made the 30-minute drive to meet our new little girl.

I'll never forget the first time I saw her. Greg, Chad, and I all walked into the room, and there she was in a bassinet, all dressed in pink. She was so tiny. So perfect. So beautiful! This was our daughter! Years of disappointment, frustration, and impatience fell by the wayside. All that mattered was her—our baby girl. Tears fell as we cradled her for the first time. We had waited so long, and worked so hard, for this moment. It seemed surreal.

The agency had a rule that we didn't like. They explained we needed to meet the baby, then go home overnight to think about it, to be absolutely sure we wanted to proceed. (After spending almost three years, thousands of dollars, and countless months of waiting—we needed to "think about it"?)

We did go home, but we didn't think about it. We had finished our thinking process years earlier. We couldn't wait to bring Bethany Brooke home the next day. But first, I had to run to the baby store to buy more adorable baby girl clothes for the current season, now that we knew she was arriving in November when the weather was cool. I also found a few other necessities (ruffled tights, little black patent leather shoes, cute onesies, lacy dresses, hats, headbands). We made sure the approved car seat was ready. We couldn't wait to shout to the whole world: "Our daughter has arrived!"

Everyone was thrilled. Many had walked the journey with us for years. Some of our closest friends knew the more painful emotions we had experienced as we tried to add to our family naturally, followed by the years of stress and work it took to jump through the adoption hoops. Don't let anyone ever tell you that adoption is easy. There are no labor contractions requiring an epidural, but an enormous amount of emotional baggage is wrapped up in this type of delivery.

Sleep eluded us that night. After hours of tossing and turning, the sun rose. This was our big day. We drove back to the agency and signed some papers. We had a new baby daughter! I kept sneaking looks in the back seat as Greg drove home, trying to convince myself this was our new reality.

We stopped at the homes of both sets of grandparents, who conveniently (for babysitting) lived nearby. We introduced them to their new granddaughter, and they happily cuddled her and welcomed her to the family.

Our best friends, who happened to live across the street, had already arranged to have a stork sign in our front yard when we finally made it home. It announced, "It's a Girl!"

Chad said something that day that still makes us chuckle. It was November 8, 1988, which was a voting day for the presidential election.

Chad said, "This is the best day of my life! Bethany Brooke arrived, and George Bush won!"

The next day, we took Bethany to Chad's third-grade class, so he could proudly hold his baby sister and show her off to everyone. The teacher graciously allowed it and smiled while observing Chad's enormous excitement and pride. He was no longer an only child; he was now a big brother.

It was an exciting but crazy season. I wasn't just preparing for the holiday season. My creative side required that I design a fun birth announcement. This was a huge milestone: the only daughter we would ever have and our last baby.

Then there were multiple baby showers. Our house took on a pink hue with all the gifts we received! I needed to send thank you notes and birth announcements on top of the 100+ Christmas cards and letters we customarily send out each year. It was a wild and exhausting time. I think I ran on adrenaline for weeks, considering the lack of sleep that comes with an infant in the house.

Bethany Brooke took it all in stride. She slept and ate and cried occasionally. She was a good baby and didn't give us much trouble at all. Just a few weeks passed until she was sleeping through the night. I dressed my little princess in pink and put Velcro bows in her little wisps of hair. I put headbands around her head that matched her outfits, even though my father was sure they were cutting off her circulation.

Our family was complete, and all was well.

Or so we thought. ♥

4

Houston, We Have a Problem

I was able to stay home for several weeks, thanks to my considerate employer and their adoption policies. When it was time to re-enter the workforce, they let me work at home part-time and occasionally bring Bethany with me when I needed to go into the office.

Time passed and Bethany grew. She was also becoming quite active, even as an infant. I have a series of three photos of her climbing up the back of our recliner at seven months old. That was a symbolic foretaste of things to come.

Her toddlerhood was fairly normal, except for her activity level. She was a mover and a shaker—go, go, and go some more. She wanted to climb everything in sight and run everywhere, never walk. She was hard to control in a store. Before Beth arrived, I would turn my nose up in judgment when I saw a parent who had their child on a "leash."

Guess who bought one? It came in handy when she was a toddler, as Beth was known to take off running in public places, and I sometimes found it hard to catch her. Oh, the humility—and patience—God was teaching me through this daughter of mine.

I quickly learned that I didn't have all the parenting expertise I thought I had. Child #1 was an easy child. He behaved as expected and responded well to discipline. Child #2 taught me that sometimes you have to throw out the parenting books.

As Beth grew into her preschool years, she continued with her high energy level. When she was three, I became concerned that she wasn't talking at a normal developmental level for her age. I had her screened at the local library when an organization held a free speech screening, and her test result came back as borderline. They wondered if she had a hearing problem, so we tested her, but it was normal. They advised me to give her a little more time and return if she didn't start talking more.

After a while, she did talk more, and she slept less. As a toddler, she had started crawling out of her crib at 18 months old. The pediatrician told us to take the crib down and put the mattress on the floor, and "make the room her crib." We did that and put a pet gate up at her doorway, which she promptly crawled over. So, we put two gates up, one on top of the other. She was able to crawl over both of them when she set her mind to it. She also crawled up her wicker diaper changing table and pulled it over on her, so that had to go, too. We laughed about it but began to realize Beth was going to challenge us far more than her brother did.

When Beth was two or three years old, she began having difficulty falling asleep. She couldn't relax. We had a bedtime routine every night. I had learned that was important, but it didn't seem to help.

I read every article or book I could find on children's sleep problems. Eventually, I began sitting in her room, sometimes even lying down with her to help her stay in bed and calm down enough to fall asleep. This was only after trying all of the book recommendations, which didn't work. Sometimes it would take an hour or more of sitting quietly with her. Sometimes I was the one who fell asleep.

I had laundry and other things to do (I worked full-time), so I often would do the bedtime routine, kiss her goodnight, and hope for the best. Most of the time, I'd hear noises and come upstairs to find her looking at books, using her nightlight. She'd jump back in bed when she heard me coming. Or, if she did manage to get to sleep, she sometimes woke up after we went to sleep, and she'd get up and roam the house. This was unacceptable. Who knows what she might get into while I was sleeping? I learned to sleep with one eye open, so to speak, always listening for noises from her. I'm still a fairly light sleeper to this day, and I credit Beth for that.

I had a little motto taped to my computer at work: "This too shall pass." I would remind myself that this was just a season. I waited impatiently for this phase of life to pass—until we could both get a regular full night of sleep. I didn't know then how long I would be waiting.

During those early years, I sent a letter to *Sesame Street Parents' Guide* after they asked for parents to submit their sleep concerns:

Dear Editor:

My daughter, Bethany, is now 3 years, 2 months old. She does not go to sleep easily. That is my major problem. Neither does she require a lot of sleep, which is also somewhat inconvenient, as far as accomplishing anything around the house goes! Bethany was a fine sleeper as an infant. The problem began when she was a toddler, maybe about 18 months old. She started getting interested in the world and decided that sleeping was for the birds.

At this time, she usually gives in and goes to sleep, on average, at about 10:30 p.m. She gets up about 7 because I work full-time, and she goes to the sitter. I almost always have to wake her in the morning. I will only allow her to take a one-hour nap after lunch (which she really seems to need) because I want her to be tired by the time bedtime arrives. We usually begin the bedtime routine at about 8:30–9:00. We do the normal things—bath, brush teeth, stories, pray, hug and kiss. She usually listens to soothing music after that, although I've tried putting her to bed without music, too.

She just has a very hard time settling down and giving in to sleep. The normal routine is for her to get out of bed as soon as I leave and play in her room. She "reads" books. She takes clothes out of her dresser and tries them on. She began climbing on top of the changing table when she was very young. She's a climber and a

Maralee Parker

mover. We tried to encourage her to stay in bed, and for a while, punished her for getting out of bed. When she was a toddler, we had to put a child gate up at her doorway, and after she immediately climbed over that, we put two gates up—one on top of the other. Eventually, she learned to climb over both of them.

Bethany also wakes up in the middle of the night at least once a night and sometimes four or five times a night. She comes to her gate and cries. Then my husband or I have to get up and encourage her to get back in bed. It takes very little time—she's usually back asleep within minutes—but it interrupts our sleep and hers. I tried to do what the experts said and let her cry, but she is a strong-willed little girl and will cry for HOURS. Our three bedrooms are close together, so the entire family is disturbed if I let this happen. It's just easier to get up and cover her and be back in bed within a minute.

Recently, I've resorted to lying down with her on top of the covers. This makes her happy and seems to help her calm down enough to get to sleep. I wonder if she may have ADHD. I know that sleep problems are a symptom of that. She is quite active during the day, too, although she can concentrate on coloring, cutting, watching TV, etc. for small periods of time.

She has always fallen asleep easily in the car while restrained in her car seat. My theory is that she knows she can't move, so she gives in and relaxes, allowing herself to fall asleep. I've thought more than once about bringing that car seat up to her room!"

I sent it off, and an editor at Sesame Street actually called me! It was exciting. We spoke, but that was the last I heard from them, although they did do a generic article about sleep in an upcoming issue of the magazine.

Birthdays three, four, and five came and went, and as they did, we saw more emotional outbursts from Beth until it was almost a daily occurrence. She was easily frustrated, then she became angry. We used a variety of discipline methods such as talking it out, time outs, removing privileges, as well as trying a positive approach, rewarding good behavior. We were not opposed to spanking and also used that, but it did no good. She didn't learn from discipline. She did what she wanted, usually very impulsively, without much thought.

One day when she was about five, she got angry about something, so I sent her to her room upstairs to cool off (so I thought). I started hearing loud noises and intense screaming coming from that direction, so I went to investigate. There she was, in the midst of her 100+ books, which she had thrown all over her room. It was my first "aha" moment. I realized we had a more serious problem on our hands. We didn't have a normal child here who was having a temper tantrum. There was much more happening, and it scared me, big time.

Here is a quote from an email I had sent a friend around that time:

> Bethany is so negative, argumentative, nasty, and sassy. She has had four what I call "rages" in the past three weeks. That's where she gets mad about something, usually when we are trying to discipline her, and goes berserk. She physically attacks, screams, cries, kicks, bites, spits, whatever she can think of. She throws things. She threw my husband's glasses into the garbage this week during one of her rages, and he is blind without them. He was sitting on the kitchen floor with her, trying to restrain her to help her calm down, and they were both absolutely exhausted after this had gone on for about 15 minutes. (Our family therapist recommended we use this 'restraining' approach.) She is so very strong-willed. She has so much energy and will not give up. And she only weighs 53 pounds. You would think we would be able to handle her physically, wouldn't you?"

We didn't know it at that time, but it was just the beginning. Thank God that He doesn't reveal the future to us.

We enrolled Beth in a private Christian school for preschool and early elementary years. I liked the small classes, personal attention, and continuation of the Biblical values we taught at home. She moved through preschool and kindergarten without much trouble, but when she was in first grade, and the work became more challenging, the teacher recommended we have her psychologically tested for ADHD (Attention Deficit Hyperactivity Disorder). I had been reading about it for several years already, thinking she might have it, so I wasn't surprised with the suggestion.

We made an appointment with a psychologist and filled out a questionnaire asking about our observations of Beth at home. Her teacher also completed a questionnaire, as requested by the doctor. The psychologist then observed Beth in her office before she made the diagnosis of ADHD and ODD (Oppositional Defiant Disorder). By this time, Beth had surpassed the "strong-willed child" description and moved into an oppositional classification where she struggled to obey us. Everything was a battle, and she was only seven years old. It was frustrating and exhausting.

We then met with a recommended psychiatrist, Dr. William Puga. It was just Beth and me who first met with him. I'll never forget that first meeting, and Dr. Puga probably won't either. We were there at least 45 minutes, and the whole time Beth did backward summersaults off the overstuffed chair. I was so glad he was able to observe her in action. We started Beth on a low dose of Ritalin after that visit. It was the first of many medications over the years.

Interestingly, Beth was not as oppositional at school. Some of my friends and family concluded that the problem must then lie with us. They thought if she could control her temper and outbursts at school, then she should be able to control them at home, too. She was just "choosing not to." When anyone hinted at that train of thought, it made me seethe! But I was pretty good at holding my tongue because I realized they had no experience with our daughter or with mental health challenges. They could hold that opinion if they chose, but I didn't want to hear it.

One night, my husband and I were out with some friends. We were in the trenches with Beth during those days and trying to hang on at the end of our rope. I was shocked when one of them said, "You don't spank her much, do you?" Perhaps my wounded, exhausted psyche was to blame for interpreting the question offensively, but it seemed to indicate we were a pair of totally incompetent parents who allowed this child to call the shots, never disciplining or teaching her correct behavior. That may not have been the intent, but that's what my brain heard. I was hurt and angry. I graciously responded that we did indeed spank, as well as give time outs, take privileges away, send her to her room, and conversely, reward for good behavior. But it seemed to all be fruitless. She just did not respond or learn from discipline.

I will never forget that conversation because it wounded my heart. These friends couldn't grasp what we were dealing with, so I assumed others would probably come to the same conclusion about our parenting skills.

In fact, another friend was extremely direct with her opinions about Beth's challenging, defiant behaviors. It affected me so much that I've kept the correspondence tucked away for years. Here's what Joanne had to say:

> I made a comment a while back that didn't really get a response, and I'm still curious what you think about it. Apparently, Beth behaves fairly well at school and around other adults and treats them well. It is only when she is at home that she acts out like this. That's the way I understand it, so correct me if I'm wrong. I just can't help but think she has you around her little finger and knows she can get away with anything she likes—so she does. This is true about normal children. I think the usual disciplining techniques for normal kids should apply to Beth: more stern discipline, make boundaries clear, consistency between parents. Now that Beth has her patterns down solid and all this behavior is well established, it would be a nightmare to change it, but she's still young enough it would be doable—with tons more work and patience.

Really, I know Beth is an extreme case, and there's a lot to it. But she's still a kid and, most of all, actually functioning in the world—she's not behind locked doors in an institute. Why wouldn't she have some behaviors and thought processes that normal kids have?

These have been my thoughts about this, and they need nurturing or ousting. If I'm wrong about all this—just slap me down!

Well! After I slapped her down, I mean after I thought about slapping her down, I tried once again to explain Beth to her. It's an almost impossible task. Unless a person has had experience living with someone with mental illness, they will never understand what parents and families face on a daily basis. These "advisors" are still using logic, and mental illness is so illogical. That's one reason it is so frustrating.

In her eyes, we needed to use more "stern discipline." Discipline did not work well with Beth. We tried several methods, and we were as consistent as we could be. I actually broke a wooden spoon over her legs once or twice (I hope the term of limitations has expired, so I'm not arrested for child abuse). We did not let her get away with things. We desperately tried to discipline her. We used time-outs repeatedly, sent her to her room to cool down, took away privileges, and had her write sentences. She sat in the time-out chair, went to her room, endured spankings, and thoroughly enjoyed earned privileges but wasn't able to apply anything she learned in order to make a better decision the next time. Nothing worked.

Here's a clip I sent to a friend in those challenging days:

I really think Bethany's Adderall wears off in the evening, and we get to enjoy her 'natural' state. It definitely is NO FUN! I have three bruises on my body to prove it. I think we need to stop the spanking, but nothing we have tried seems to help her obey. She just refuses. Argh!

We went to family counseling during this period, and as I briefly mentioned earlier, the therapist recommended we "restrict" Beth physically when she had meltdowns and rages. He told us to sit on the floor, put our arms around her, and just hold her to restrict her kicking, hitting, and biting. We tried that. I couldn't do it. I wasn't strong enough to control this eight-year-old, who was incredibly strong. She was one big muscle, especially when her adrenaline was pumping. My husband tried to restrict her (after all, we were told to do it!) a few times, but it seemed to just make her rage *more* intense. It wasn't solving anything, but it sure was leaving all three of us exhausted, physically and emotionally.

So we tried a positive approach by using a reward system. We marked charts on the fridge for good behavior with rewards in place when Beth complied with the requirements. We were met with little success. She was impulsive, distractible, hyperactive, and angry—with several sensory issues to boot. She lived with a boatload of challenges every moment of her young life. Neither discipline nor a reward system seemed to help.

By this time, we were clueless as to how to deal with her. We were willing to try medication to help her (and thus us). Here's a paragraph from my journal:

> We went to a psychiatrist for medication. We're still working with him. It's taking a long time to find what works for her. First, we tried only antidepressants (Pamelor) because Beth tends to be anxious and has always had sleep problems. That helped some but didn't produce the results her teacher or we were hoping for. We rated it a 5 out of 10.
>
> Then we tried Adderall, a stimulant; one at 7:30, one at 3:30. We worked up to 10 mg in the morning. That is what kept her up until 1 a.m. four nights that first week! So, we quickly changed that. Then we tried using just the morning dose. She was awful at night. Then we added an antidepressant after dinner (Tofranil) and still saw limited progress. Then we doubled the antidepressant to 50 mg after dinner, and that's where we are now. We see the doctor again this Thursday (and I can't wait). It is NOT working.

Maralee Parker

We were doing everything we could think of: medication, counseling, searching for answers in books and online and asking God for help. Some people observing our situation still found it easy to cast judgment. Oh, how easy it was to judge when they had never walked a mile in our shoes. I tried to remain gracious toward people who seemed to judge us because I realized we all judge. We use our limited knowledge to form opinions—too quickly.

We need to remember to think before we speak and pray for grace and mercy before casting judgment on those around us. We don't know all the details in a situation. God encourages us in James 1:19: "Understand this, my dear brothers and sisters: You must all be quick to listen, slow to speak, and slow to get angry." Quick to listen and slow to speak. We'd all do better if we listened more and talked less. I say this, but I know I am as guilty as the next person.

One day I received this email, and it meant the world to me. I saved it to read again and again:

> I've been thinking about you and just wanted to write and say that I totally admire you for your patience and tenacity and innovation and humor and love and much more through some difficult things in your life. I was bragging on you to someone yesterday about how you have gone the distance with Beth and so often laid aside your own self and made her your priority. Just wanted you to know that I have been watching from afar, and so have many others, I'm sure. You are a testimony for Christ in an unusual circumstance. Thank you!

How encouraging that was and still is. It's salve to a hurting heart!

Beth had more going on in her brain than just ADHD and ODD, as you'll learn in upcoming pages. She did her best to fit in at school, doing what she had to do, and doing everything she could to not draw attention to herself. She was timid and very anxious, and if she misbehaved, that would draw attention, which she did not want. So, she quietly sat at her desk, in her own little world, not paying attention to what was being said. The teachers worked hard to help her learn and keep pace with the rest of the class. I also worked hard at home, spending hours on homework with her almost every night, trying to help her understand and meet the requirements.

She did live in her own little world. Her attention span was short, and she didn't seem to understand interpersonal relationships. She didn't know how to be a friend, although she wanted friends.

I came across this sweet story, written by her in second grade, which illustrates her desire for friendship. The instructions from her teacher said, "On a cold day after school, you decide you'd like some hot chocolate. How would you make it? Tell how in five or six sentences." Below is her story, as written:

After school I went home and I made a snowman with my friends Sarah Courtney and Katie. Then we had a snowball fight. It was fun. Then I asked if Sarah Courtney and Katie could stay over night at my house. My mom sied yes. Ther mom sied yes too. So we went in my house and my mom was making hot cocoa. Then my mom sied that we could play for a little wile. So we did and it was fun. Soon mom called us and sied it was time for bed. When we were tucked in I sied to Sarah Courtney and Katie You are my best friends ever and Jesus is too. Then I sied to myself this is the best day of my life. The End.

Then she realized she didn't follow the instructions. She hadn't explained how to make the hot chocolate. So she squeezed this above the original story:

How to make hot cocoa. Get a glasse of milk and put some chocolate in it and put it in the mikerwave then you drink it.

Done! It made me chuckle, but it also conveyed how much she dreamed of having friends, and that made me sad for her.

(Beth has always been a good writer. She has a great imagination and can express herself quite well. That always makes me smile because I enjoy writing, too. Even though she's adopted, she somehow "caught" the writing bug. It's so satisfying!)

So, even though school was growing increasingly difficult, she hung in there, month after month, doing her best to keep up, with the help of the teachers and her ever-lovin' mama. She passed first, second, and third grades.

Though Beth was often angry and oppositional, she also had her sweet moments. When I looked past her issues, I could see that she loved me, her dad, and her brother, although she could rarely demonstrate it. I knew she was emotionally clinging to me with all her might, even while acting like she didn't care. She gave me this simple yet profound note when she was in third grade:

Dear Mom

I love you. And I hope you hav a marry Cristmas. I'm glad you adopted me becase if you did not then I whold not have a mom. I love you vary much!

My heart melted. It was that note, and other rare ones, that kept me going through the difficult years when she wouldn't let me hug or touch her and shared little affection toward me or any of us in the family. That's why I still have every one of those notes safely tucked away.

When she was in fourth grade, another day of reckoning came. It was a huge turning point.

The school principal wanted to meet with me. *Now what?* When I went in, the principal lovingly and patiently explained that the small private Christian school felt they couldn't meet Beth's educational needs any longer. They had tried. I knew how they had tried, and I was so very grateful. But in the upper elementary grades, more independent work is required, and Beth was just not able to keep up. The principal recommended that we transfer her to public school for fifth grade, where more resources would be available. I knew they were speaking truth, but still, it was so hard to hear. I wanted her to be normal, and I had done everything I could to help her stay on course. Now the principal was saying Beth needed special help, more than one teacher could provide while attending to all of the other kids in the class. I understood, but it meant a new chapter would be starting for Beth in the fall—public school. I hoped the principal was right. I hoped Beth would be able to get more help to become the best Beth she could be.

As we worked on finishing fourth grade, she still struggled with getting enough sleep at night. This challenge had gone on since she was two or three years old. She was 10 by this time, so we'd both been sleep-deprived for seven years. Yawn!

Here's an excerpt from my journal from around that time:

Thursday, Feb. 20, 1997:
Put Bethany to bed about 8:45. She did not go to sleep. When my bedtime came, I stayed with her to try to help her relax, and she finally gave in, at 11:20. I was probably with her from 10:45–11:20.

Friday, Feb. 21, 1997:
Put her to bed about 9. I scolded her a couple of times about going to sleep after that, as I heard noises upstairs. I finally decided to go to my room upstairs and work on homework, hoping that my presence would keep her in bed, allowing her to relax. [I worked full-time and was also a full-time student in an accelerated bachelor's degree completion program.]

Saturday, Feb. 22, 1997:
Put her down at 9. Encouraged her to "choose" to go to sleep, telling her she would be able to stay overnight at friends' homes and have them stay overnight here once she learned to go to sleep when she was supposed to. I came downstairs, encouraged.

9:30: Looked up the stairs to see her light on. Scolded her.

10:00: Looked up the stairs to see her light on again. Went up and gave her a spanking.

10:25: As I sat downstairs, working at the computer, I hear noises and look over to see Beth sneaking around in the dining room! She runs upstairs. I follow and give her another spanking. She yells at me, "Brat! I hate you!" She screams. She's very angry. I told her that she knows the rules, and when she breaks them, she gets a spanking.

Oct. 9, 1997:
Beth continues to struggle with sleeping. I have been lying down with her most nights again, just to keep her in bed, to help her remain quiet, and relax long enough to grow tired and fall asleep. I counted her moves the other night—she moves every three seconds. She moves something on her body every three seconds; if she's perfectly still for more than 10 seconds, I know that's a good sign. It is so very hard for her to relax!

Lately, we go upstairs at 8:30; brush teeth, go to the bathroom, read a short story if there's time, pray, and try to turn lights out by 9. I often lie there until 9:30, 10:00, or 10:15. Lately I have gotten up after a while, because I have still have my homework to do. Then she's usually still awake when I go up to bed around 11 or midnight. Sleep does not come easily for Bethany Brooke Parker.

Feb. 16, 1998:
Tomorrow is a significant day. I will finally finish my accelerated B.A. degree that I've been working so hard at for sixteen months. Every Tuesday night I've attended school for four hours, with much homework to do each week between classes. It's been a long 16 months, especially with Beth's special needs. But it's over now. I did it! I am so relieved it's over.

Beth's struggle with sleep continued night after night, year after year (and still continues, to this day). Finally, when she was about 12 years old, I decided I was done. I came to realize if she had to get up in the middle of the night and wander around the house, then that was her decision. She would be the one who would be tired the next day. As for me, I needed my sleep. I decided she was old enough to be safe in the house and didn't need me to nag her anymore. The "Sleep Patrol" officially resigned, and I've never looked back.

Let's get back to Beth's school transition. She started her career in public school in fifth grade. I wanted to help pave the way to make the transition easier. Beth didn't do well with change, and this one was huge. I wrote a creative four-page summary, with pictures, of "who Beth is" and gave it to the education team. It started with an acrostic poem, using her name:

Beautiful, curly hair ... naturally! (If only it got washed more often.)

Energetic at home ... rarely walks anywhere; usually runs. Runs on all fours around the house when she's not on Ritalin.

True and loyal friend after she puts her trust in someone. She's a one-person-at-a-time friend, however.

Happy when she feels emotionally "safe" and not threatened. I love to hear her laugh.

Adores Daniel Radcliffe, the actor who plays Harry Potter. Her life revolves around him; she knows much trivia about him and the Harry Potter series.

Night owl. Sleeps very little! Since she was 18 months old ... sleep to Beth has been something to be avoided.

Yearns to be "normal" like other kids, yet realizes she's not. This makes her sad. And sometimes mad.

Even though the new school was conveniently located a few blocks from home (no more chauffeuring to a school miles away), it was a larger school, with more rules, more kids, and more noise. She was fearful, but I encouraged her, reassuring her she would make a friend and it would be fine. The staff tested her and assigned her a "collaborative interventionist" to help her. They provided a checklist to help her get her homework home. I had to sign off on it each night, and then it would be checked by the interventionist the next morning. This helped the communication a great deal between school and home.

One of the first challenges in public school began with this "collaborative interventionist," who was concerned that Beth wasn't getting all of her homework done. I remember the day the C.I. called me at work to scold me (that's how it felt) because Beth didn't get everything done every night. *Excuse me?* I thought to myself, my indignation immediately rising as she spoke.

Those who know me would tell you I am usually a stable, calm, non-reactionary person. But this phone call ticked me off! I carefully explained, with measured words, that I sat with my daughter for one or two hours (and sometimes more) every night, trying to encourage her and help her focus to get the assignments done. It was a daunting task. Beth didn't understand that if she would "apply herself" (such great *educationese*), she would be free to go play instead of sit at the table for hours. My years of experience with her helped me understand she just couldn't do it. This time it wasn't a matter of showing defiance. So, we struggled. And struggled! And here I was—trying to explain our daughter's behavior to this interventionist, which was difficult because it wasn't logical. I felt I was being yelled at for not measuring up, and I knew my husband and I were putting all we had into helping Beth succeed. I had no emotional reserves left to deal with it.

So, in a very un-Maralee type of response, I called the principal. I laugh now because that is so not me. I hate drama. I can put up with a lot—a boatload—of frustration. But in this situation, I called the principal to express my concern about this person who, I felt, verbally attacked me. The principal was kind, diplomatic, and understanding, and I felt much better after explaining my concerns.

I soon got a call from the C.I., who said something like, "I'm sorry you were offended by my call." It wasn't exactly what I was looking for, but I let bygones be bygones. Then a miracle happened. There have been many miracles in Beth's life. This is one of them.

Brenda, the C.I., and I became great friends! She and Beth and I began working together in earnest, and that more cooperative, understanding alliance helped make the difficult homework requirement more attainable. Assignments were adjusted for her. We still didn't always get everything done, but the understanding and communication helped so much.

A Work Completion Plan was typed up, which the school and I agreed upon. It said Beth should "work no more than 20 minutes on any subject per night. Bethany must be working for the entire 20 minutes, not daydreaming or refusing to work."

Yes, that was the goal, but I was not a miracle worker! There was an entire typewritten page of rewards and consequences if she did do the work and if she didn't. We tried. Things were better, but this by no means solved the problem.

Christmas was approaching by this time, and in Sunday school, Beth and her class made invitations to the children's Christmas program at church. The kids were encouraged to invite people. So, to my amazement, Beth, my very shy and anxious girl, invited Brenda! Even more amazing—Brenda came and brought a friend! I was astounded.

When I had kidney cancer surgery, Brenda brought flowers and visited me in the hospital. She and I became email friends. She gave me books about ADHD and sensory issues. I shared my faith journey with her along the way, and it inspired her own faith to the point where she decided to get baptized—and invited us! She invited us to other social events, and we did the same. We had become friends. I am so thankful for Brenda. God has sent many angels throughout Beth's life to bless us both, and this one's name was Brenda. ♥

5

The Struggle Is Real

By this time, Beth was 10 or 11 years old, and her emotional outbursts had been happening regularly for several years. We felt like we had to continually walk on eggshells around her, never sure what would set her off. When she lost it, she could not control herself. We just had to live through it, waiting for it to pass. I, especially, had to be very careful because Beth became physically combative and would kick, hit, pinch, and even bite me when she was raging. I think she only bit me a few times, but I had the bite marks to prove it. I had scratches and bruises on my arms and legs, off and on, for years. Beth would forget the event as soon as it was over while I limped on, trying to emotionally recuperate from the battles. She always took her rage out on me. The only time she hit her dad was if he was trying to protect me.

As I described the weekly and sometimes daily meltdown experiences with my closest girlfriends, they would listen sympathetically, hardly believing the stories I told. They often said, "I don't know how you do it." Sometimes they didn't know how to respond. As I continued to share, they came to understand this was our reality. They listened to me vent and prayed. I coveted their support and prayers and felt we wouldn't survive if God wasn't giving us the strength and wisdom to persevere, one day at a time.

Much love and gratitude go to my buddies who listened (and read my emails) again and again and again—and lifted us in prayer. You know who you are. You were the hands and feet of Jesus for me during those years. Thank you!

We didn't know what the answer was. We loved Beth. She was a sweet, shy girl when she wasn't angry. We had committed to loving her and raising her, and we weren't going to change our minds or give her back. (That wasn't an option.) As followers of Jesus, we knew He had a plan for our lives, as Jeremiah 29:11 states, "For I know the plans I have for you," says the Lord. "They are plans for good and not for disaster, to give you a future and a hope." Romans 8:28 also served as a reminder. "And we know that God causes everything to work together for the good of those who love God and are called according to his purpose for them."

We trust God. We love Him, have committed our lives to Him, and even when we don't understand, we trust in His wisdom and purpose. So, as we were going through the hard years, we reminded ourselves that we just needed to hold on to Jesus, our anchor, and as the Disney character, Dory says, "Just keep swimming. Just keep swimming."

That's what we did. We lived our lives the best we could, one day at a time. We confronted challenging situations as they arose, doing the best we could. It was not pretty. It was extremely difficult. It became more challenging when Beth was in her teens and early twenties.

Many marriages suffer when there is mental illness in the home, often ending in divorce. We firmly believe in working to keep a marriage strong but admit that it gets really difficult when you have the challenges of mental illness added to the normal challenges every married couple faces. With mental illness, life is not in your control. You just have to roll with it and do the best you can. And pray. Ask God for help. Tell Him all about it, spend time in the Bible, and claim the promises you find there. Our faith helped us endure the many years of pain and uncertainty we went through in raising our girl. Thank You for your faithfulness, God!

Divorce was not an option. That was something we felt strongly about from the beginning of our marriage. It's good to make that decision before you and your spouse are in the midst of challenges where you can barely keep your heads above water.

Greg and I look back sometimes and laugh again at our response when the social worker asked us, "Would you be willing to accept a baby with special needs?" We confidently responded that we were not cut out for that. We had our careers, after all. We were busy and didn't have time to devote to a baby with special needs.

We plan, and God laughs. And now, 33 years later, we laugh, too. We couldn't laugh as we were going through it. That was when the tears came. We can trace the hand of God in our lives with the added benefit of hindsight.

Greg worked long hours providing for his family. He now admits that part of it was because he didn't want to be around the conflict. After all, he couldn't fix it. Men want to fix problems. Since there was no easy fix to our situation, he wanted to avoid it and did, to a great extent, by working many hours each week. He freely admits that now. Greg was an amazing provider, but it was me who dealt with Beth much of the time. I raised Beth.

I was very thankful for our next-door neighbor, Kailey, who was Beth's age. They played together, at least in their younger years. Beth didn't know how to have a reciprocal relationship with give and take. She wanted it but couldn't do it. Kailey wanted someone to play with, and Beth was right there, so they did spend some fun times together.

Without many friends, she grew quite dependent on me while pushing me away at the same time. As she grew older, she realized she needed me to help her get through life, to help her understand what was expected of her. She continued to be very anxious and shy and couldn't talk to people. For example, I had to order for her in a restaurant for many years, even into young adulthood. Sometimes I'd say, "What was it you wanted, Beth?" to try to encourage her to interact. But usually, she would tell me what she wanted, and I'd order. She didn't feel comfortable paying the cashier in a store either. Those social interactions with people were very stressful for her. She had anxiety about many things in life.

And then she got another diagnosis. ♥

6

When You've Seen One Aspie, You've Seen One Aspie

After being diagnosed with ADHD and ODD, Beth started medication, and the three of us participated in family counseling. We were willing to do whatever we could to help Beth and our family's life, too.

I read books on ADHD and spirited children. I attended some meetings sponsored by a group called CHADD (Children and Adults with Attention-Deficit/Hyperactivity Disorder) to learn tips for raising a kid like Beth. I signed up for a couple of online support groups to learn from other parents or, at the very least, learn that I was not alone in raising a challenging child. We compared notes, asked questions, and exchanged war stories. It was such a help knowing that someone else understood the journey. Even when there are no easy answers, it helps to know others truly do get it. (If you're interested, in your browser, search "online support groups for ADHD" or whatever challenge you need support for, and you'll often find many options. Facebook also has many support groups.)

When Beth was 12, and in sixth grade, our family therapist suggested Beth get tested again to ensure we knew what we were treating. Although it's not an exact science, I believe in psychological testing. I will never forget when the psychologist gave us the new results.

"It's very clear. Beth's tests indicate she has high-functioning autism. It's called Asperger's syndrome."

I was shocked. I hadn't seen that coming because I was busy with her ADHD, sleep challenges, oppositional behaviors, sensory issues, and

Maralee Parker

anxiety. I didn't know we had room for another diagnosis.

I started researching autism, specifically Asperger's syndrome. A few years ago, Asperger's syndrome was taken out of the DSM-5 (Diagnostic and Statistical Manual of Mental Disorders). People with any type of autism are now diagnosed as being on the autism spectrum, including kids and adults who are nonverbal and those who are highly verbal with high intelligence. They all are diagnosed with ASD, or autism spectrum disorder, although many people still choose to use the term Asperger's. It does seem to define the higher functioning type of ASD better.

As I researched, I learned that there were big tip-offs for ASD, such as trouble with social skills, communicating with others, being able to look someone directly in the eyes instead of avoiding eye contact. Obsessions with a particular object or subject were also characteristic of autism. Beth had them all.

She had difficulty since she was a preschooler in making friends. She has also always had challenges with motor skills and loved routine. That's a positive way of putting it. In other words, she had a meltdown if things didn't go the way she was anticipating. Flexibility and transitioning were very difficult for her. All of these things were characteristics of autism.

Beth wasn't what I'd call a typical *aspie* (slang for someone with Asperger's). Often, aspies are quite socially inept but can rattle off a multitude of details about their specific obsession. They know many facts but can't read emotion in a person's face or know appropriate things to say to have a typical conversation.

Beth had obsessions since she was a preschooler. She was extremely interested in her obsession but wasn't interested in much else. The first one was whales. Whales, whales, whales. Then Scooby-Doo, the cartoon character. When she was older, it was the movie *Titanic*. I think we watched it 50+ times. Then followed the historical Eastland Disaster—the sinking of a ship in the Chicago River in 1915. She was totally into the *Free Willy* movies. Then Pokémon. One of her longest-lasting obsessions was animated Japanese shows (anime), which she still enjoys. She loved the *Sailor Moon* anime TV show. (When she was over 18, she had a huge *Sailor Moon* character tattooed on her shoulder.) She was in love with Ryo, a Ronan Warrior anime character. She "talked" to him on TV and wrote stories about the characters called "fan fics." Hundreds of stories. She printed out color pictures of these characters from the internet, using many ink cartridges. Most parents would have put a stop to that ink expense. But by that time, we were already into the "whatever works" lifestyle. She had no friends, no hobbies, no activities, and had deepening depression. Letting her print out her pictures and stories made her happier and gave her something to do. A few ink cartridges were worth the cost of keeping her content and purposeful for a while.

Following that, her obsession turned to Harry Potter (we saw it 10 times in the theater), then it was Lord of the Rings (saw it five times). She loved fantasy and loved to escape into it. While we didn't encourage it, we could do little to avoid it. These obsessions, and sometimes fantasies, took over her life.

Many kids and adults with Asperger's tend to fit with the "walking encyclopedia" description. They are often extremely intelligent, with expert-level knowledge about their obsessions, but they lack social skills. Beth was different. Her IQ was below normal, which explains why she had trouble with daily living skills such as counting money, adding and subtracting (you can forget multiplication), and following a series of directions. She could handle one or maybe two directions at a time before becoming overwhelmed and confused.

She had trouble looking someone in the eye when talking or listening, and her conversations with anyone outside of family were very brief. However, there were times when she amazed me and basically made a liar out of me after I'd explained to someone ahead of time "how Beth is." I loved when that happened.

I came across this quote when I was researching Asperger's: "When you've seen one aspie, you've seen one aspie." The syndrome is not cookie-cutter. A person who is diagnosed can be very different from another with the same diagnosis. Maybe that's why it's called the "autism spectrum."

From my years of studying mental illness, I've learned about the overlap in symptoms from one illness to another. It's called comorbidity. Anxiety, for example, is found in many mental illness diagnoses. Sensory challenge is another common co-morbid symptom. It's also common to have extreme reactions to a change in plans or difficulty transitioning from one activity to another.

Buying clothes for this unique child of mine was challenging as well. Trying on clothes in a store dressing room didn't work with her sensory issues, social issues, and impatience. She would become increasingly agitated as she tried them on because they had to feel just right. If they didn't, she became frustrated and angry. After trying that "normal" approach to clothes shopping a few times and realizing it was not working, I developed my own plan. Take jeans, for example. I'd pick out a few different jean styles in sizes I thought might work, bring them home, and help her decide which fit best and felt comfortable after trying them on in the comfort of our own home. Then I'd return the rest and buy three pairs of the ones that worked. It was exhausting, but the plan provided clothes that fit until she grew out of them. Then we would repeat the process.

Celebrating her birthday with the family was also unique. As she grew to be nine or ten, we learned we shouldn't sing "Happy Birthday," have her blow out candles, or open presents at the party. She greatly anticipated her "party" with family coming over, but she couldn't handle the stress of being the center of attention. After everyone left, she had fun opening her presents. I think most of the family understood the situation and why it was best to go with the flow. Greg and I had long given up our expectations for "normal," and most of the family was learning to do it as well, little by little.

Here is a holiday letter I found years ago on an autism website, written by Viki Gayhardt—singer, songwriter, and parent of two children with autism. Maybe it will be helpful in understanding someone on the autism spectrum:

Dear Family and Friends,

I understand that we will be visiting each other for the holidays this year! Sometimes these visits can be very hard for me, but here is some information that might help our visit to be more successful. As you probably know, I am challenged by a hidden disability called Autism, or what some people refer to as a Pervasive Developmental Disorder (PDD). Autism/PDD is a neurodevelopmental disorder which makes it hard for me to understand the environment around me. I have barriers in my brain that you can't see, but which make it difficult for me to adapt to my surroundings.

Sometimes I may seem rude and abrupt, but it is only because I have to try so hard to understand people and at the same time, make myself understood. People with autism have different abilities: some may not speak, some write beautiful poetry. Others are whizzes in math (Albert Einstein was thought to be autistic), or may have difficulty making friends. We are all different and need various degrees of support.

Sometimes when I am touched unexpectedly, it might feel painful and make me want to run away. I get easily frustrated, too. Being with lots of other people is like standing next to a moving freight train and trying to decide how and when to jump aboard. I feel frightened and confused a lot of the time. This is why I need to have things the same as much as possible. Once I learn how things happen, I can get by OK. But if something, anything, changes, then I have to relearn the situation all over again! It is very hard.

When you try to talk to me, I often can't understand what you say because there is a lot of distraction around. I have to concentrate very hard to hear and understand one thing at a time. You might think I am ignoring you—I am not. Rather, I am hearing everything and not knowing what is most important to respond to.

Holidays are exceptionally hard because there are so many different people, places, and things going on that are out of my ordinary realm. This may be fun and adventurous for most people, but for me, it's very hard work and can be extremely stressful. I often have to get away from all the commotion to calm down. It would be great if you had a private place set up to where I could retreat.

If I cannot sit at the meal table, do not think I am misbehaved or that my parents have no control over me. Sitting in one place for even five minutes is often impossible for me. I feel so antsy and overwhelmed by all the smells, sounds, and people—I just have to get up and move about. Please don't hold up your meal—go on without me, and my parents will handle the situation the best way they know how.

Eating in general is hard for me. If you understand that autism is a sensory processing disorder, it's no wonder eating is a problem! Think of all the senses involved with eating. Sight, smell, taste, touch, AND all the complicated mechanics that are involved. Chewing and swallowing is something that a lot of people with autism have trouble with. I am not being picky—I literally cannot eat certain foods as my sensory system and/or oral motor coordination are impaired.

Don't be disappointed if Mom hasn't dressed me in starch and bows. It's because she knows how much stiff and frilly clothes can drive me buggy! I have to feel comfortable in my clothes or I will just be miserable. When I go to someone else's house, I may appear bossy and controlling. In a sense, I am being controlling, because that is how I try to fit into the world around me (which is so hard to figure out!). Things have to be done in a way I am familiar with or else I might get confused and frustrated. It doesn't mean you have to change the way you are doing things—just please be patient with me, and understanding of how I have to cope. Mom and Dad have no control over how my autism makes me feel inside. People with autism often have little things that they do to help themselves feel more comfortable. The grown-ups call it "self-regulation," or "stimming." I might rock, hum, flick my fingers, or any number of different things. I am not trying to be disruptive or weird. Again, I am doing what I have to do for my brain to adapt to your world. Sometimes I cannot stop myself from talking, singing, or doing an activity I enjoy. The grown-ups call this "perseverating," which is kind of like self-regulation or stimming. I do this only because I have found something to occupy myself that makes me feel comfortable. Perseverative behaviors are good to a certain degree, because they help me calm down.

Please be respectful to my mom and dad if they let me "stim" for a while as they know me best and what helps to calm me. Remember that my mom and dad have to watch me much more closely than the average child. This is for my own safety, and preservation of your possessions. It hurts my parents' feelings to be criticized for being overprotective, or condemned for not watching me close enough. They are human and have been given an assignment intended for saints. My parents are good people and need your support.

Holidays are filled with sights, sounds, and smells. The average household is turned into a busy, frantic, festive place. Remember that this may be fun for you, but it's very hard work for me to conform. If I fall apart or act out in a way that you consider socially inappropriate, please remember that I don't possess the neurological system that is required to follow some social rules. I am a unique person—an interesting person. I will find my place at

Maralee Parker

this Celebration that is comfortable for us all, as long as you'll try to view the world through my eyes!"

Sometimes Beth could not find her place at family celebrations. All she wanted to do was go home. Sometimes when celebrations were held at our home, she would stay in her room—her safe place. We learned, over time, to just go with the flow and let her be comfortable. We let go of our "Hallmark Christmas" expectations and accepted what it was—totally unpredictable.

Sometimes I would struggle with why she acted the way she did. Why couldn't she just cooperate and do what was expected? Her behaviors were often puzzling, even for me, who knew her better than anyone. Then I'd be reminded of something I had written in her baby book when she was five:

> Bethany has strong opinions. She also sounds like she has a doctorate in psychology sometimes. There's a simple line she uses often, and it makes a lot of sense. When I tell her to do something, something she disagrees with, like "Button up your coat or you'll be cold," she says, "You don't know, because you're not me!"

You're right, Beth. We're not you. We will spend our lives doing everything we can to help you, but we'll never fully understand because we are not you.

By the time she was in sixth grade, Beth had received three diagnoses: ADHD, ODD, and now Asperger's syndrome. It seemed we were collecting diagnoses. Would there be more? ♥

7

Our Happy Place

In 2000, when Beth was 12, Chad became engaged to a lovely girl named Melissa. Greg and I decided we wanted to plan a "final family vacation" before Chad flew the coop. We agreed that Melissa could come, too, since she was almost part of the family.

Four of us greatly anticipated our trip to Walt Disney World that summer. After all, it is "the most magical place on Earth," right? But Beth grew antsier and antsier about it. I think she sensed our anticipation and grew increasingly anxious as the big day approached. Most people relish a change of scenery, but it terrified Beth. She knew her little, safe world was going to be shaken up for a week.

She made a list of things she thought she needed to take. Here it is, exactly as she typed it:

1. POEM ABOUT ADOPTION (MABEY)
2. LULLUBY TRAIN (MAYBY)
3. GREEN SQOURT
4. FLOOWER JEEN SQUORT
5. TK
6. PERIL
7. JUPIE
8. SHIRTS
9. SWIM SUTE
10. SHORTS
11. DIGIMON MAGAZINES
12. FOXIEMON
13. PAGAMAS

14. JELLY PENS
15. DIARY
16. BRACLET
17. DIGIMON SCRAPBOOK
18. PINK STRAW HAT
19. CAMRA
20. TOWAL
21. PICTERS OF MATT
22. ANY DIGIMON CARDS
23. PILLOW
24. SLEEPING BAG
25. PICTERS OF MY FRIENDS
26. BOOKS
27. SOKES
28. SHOES
29. POOH BEAR HAT
30. BIBLE
31. FRIENDSHIP STUFF TO REMEMBER MY FRIENDS
32. A BAG IN CASE I GET CAR SICK AND THROW UP
33. UNDERWEAR
34. CD'S
35. SUMTHING TO HOLD CLAM SHELLS, SHELLS, AND SNALE SHELLS
36. DRINKS SO I WON'T GET DIHIDERATED FROM THE SUN AND FOR OTHER STUFF.

She was quite thorough, don't you think? There was a theme going there with Digimon, one of her current anime obsessions at the time. I was encouraged she had "Bible" on the list, although I don't think it made it into her suitcase.

We went on the trip, and we made it back home. We survived. It was a trip none of us will ever forget. Following is the email I sent out to close friends, as I summarized our Florida experience, so I wouldn't have to repeat it a dozen times. It begins as we were loading up the van to leave:

Bethany has a hard time with transitions. She was NOT excited about this trip and was having a hard time leaving her good friend, Lisa, and leaving her special TV shows. We kept prodding her toward this trip for weeks, actually, trying to get her prepared, and she had made encouraging comments like she was moving in the right direction. But on the morning of departure, she was NOT acting very excited. She was watching TV as we busily loaded everything. We had planned to leave at 9 am. Greg was finally ready at 10 am. Beth was not ready, and Greg told us all to get in the van (as in "he would take care of Bethany"). The next thing we knew, Beth was running out the door, screaming, throwing all her stuff on the sidewalk and vanishing into the backyard. Greg went after her and grabbed her and tried to physically put her in the van, and got bites and bruises from that as she let off a list of expletives. She is like a wild animal when she loses control like this. Suffice it to say that it took another hour, prayer, and psychological expertise from Chad and then myself to ease, ease, ease her back to the house from her escape place, down the creek bed behind our house (she was covered with mud on her legs). We then had to gather more things from the house she thought she had to have (way more than she needed, but it's a psychological thing, it was "safety and security" to her) and get her in the car. We left about 11 am—emotionally exhausted!

Whew. It was not a pretty sight. And that is how our vacation began. We finally arrived in Orlando the next day, after staying in a hotel overnight along the way. We got settled into our rental unit, and the next morning brought our first day to venture out. Chad and Melissa went to visit a relative of Melissa's that day, while Greg and Beth and I went to Disney's Animal Kingdom. We figured that might be a better and safer place to start for Beth since she loved animals. And the email continues:

Animal Kingdom is a big place! It was HOT. But fun! I absolutely loved the "It's Tough to be a Bug" 3-D show. It was so cute and so much fun. Looks like the bugs and other things are directly in front of your face. We went on the safari ride, the raft splash thing (yes, we got soaked), saw The Lion King show, etc. A fun day, except we had to encourage and prod Beth all day long to go from activity to activity. She usually enjoyed each thing after she got there but whined about going home (back to the condo) all day long—ugh.

Monday, we all went to SeaWorld. We had a wonderful experience there 10 years ago and were looking forward to seeing it again. We love feeding the stingrays and dolphins. One fun moment in the day was when I was holding my little dead sardine up, waiting for Greg to take my picture, when a tricky little seagull flew right over and grabbed it out of my hand!

Unfortunately, while we were feeding the rays, Chad asked Beth to move over (he was videotaping), and she didn't like it, and that little thing set her off. She went stomping off in the opposite direction. This is not a good idea at a theme park where there are thousands of people walking around. We sent Chad and Melissa off by themselves and arranged to meet at a show. It took Bethany a full hour to come around again and act somewhat "normal." It was very stressful for Greg and me, trying to keep track of where she was, without her knowing it ... it's that oppositional thing ... until she could emotionally let go and come back and join us.

Things went better for the next couple of hours, and then we had another similar incident at the Shamu Stadium. It's huge. People everywhere. There's just no reasoning with her when she melts down, and she gets "set off" by the stupidest things. It really was spoiling the experience for the rest of us. This last meltdown came later at night, like 7 pm, and the park was getting ready to close. We tried to give her space, but we had to keep our eye on her! She finally recovered and decided to join us and talk to me, and we eventually made it to the tram, and then back to our van. She was much better then, relieved, I think, to be back in familiar territory. We were ALL relieved to be back in the van and headed toward the condo. It had been a very stressful day.

Greg and I talked it over that night and made the decision that Chad, Melissa, and I would do the Disney parks by ourselves, and he and Beth would stay at the condo. They could swim in the pool, read, and watch TV (remember, she is somewhat obsessive about TV, too).

So, on Tuesday, Chad, Melissa, and I went to Epcot and walked and walked and walked (and drank and sweated; repeat). It's a beautiful place! We had a great time. Beth and Greg did just fine, too. She was perfectly content to stay at the condo, and Greg wasn't too disappointed by it either. He loves to read and isn't thrilled by amusement parks. It all worked out.

On Wednesday, we went to Daytona Beach and enjoyed riding the waves in the Atlantic. It was so much fun! While we were out in about four feet of water, we actually saw stingrays swimming right in front of us. That was freaky! In fact, Chad decided he really didn't like the ocean so much anymore, but Melissa, Beth, and I just stayed there.

The waves near the shore knocked me down twice. When they crashed, they were incredibly powerful. Out deeper, it's just fun to go with them and ride the waves. It was a great day for everyone.

On the way home, Chad got to take a tour through Daytona Speedway, which he loved.

The big laugh for the day? The guys thought it was hilarious that Melissa and I had talked about wanting to watch a sunset on the ocean. They explained that we would be waiting a very long time for the sun to "set" on the Atlantic. In fact, we'd be waiting until the sun rose the next morning!

On Thursday, the three of us went to Universal Studios, and on Friday, we headed off to the Magic Kingdom and had a blast. Part of me felt really guilty that we were enjoying ourselves while Beth and Greg were back at the condo, but Greg reassured me that it was FINE. Beth was definitely not upset about staying there. She's just not "normal." What kid wouldn't love Disney World? We learned the hard way; it was too stimulating and stressful for her.

On Saturday, we left the condo at 6 a.m. and drove for 20 hours, pulling into our driveway at 2 a.m. We drove the last five hours through rain and fog. But it was so good to be back home. Good to get away (for four of us), wonderful to come back (for all five of us)!

It was quite the vacation to remember—in more ways than one. In hindsight, we could have handled Beth's anxiety and transition troubles in better ways. We are not perfect parents; this is for certain. Beth had complained that Chad got to bring a friend, but she didn't, and she felt that was unfair. Melissa was almost family, and our Villager minivan was already packed with five people plus luggage. There was no room for a sixth passenger. But perhaps I could have bribed Beth (I was not above that!), promising her and her best friend a special event when we returned, to give her something to look forward to and help her feel like we weren't favoring Chad by allowing him to bring Melissa. But I hadn't thought of that option. It might have helped.

Typical vacations didn't work out so well for Beth, as you probably surmised. The anxiety of the unknown made it difficult for her to relax and enjoy a vacation. It also made it difficult for the rest of the family to relax and enjoy a vacation.

So, we found a different answer called Sandy Pines Recreational Community. It's a resort in southwest Michigan, in the middle of nowhere. My best friend's family had invested in a place there and loved it. They invited our family for a visit every summer. It was a wonderful place to relax, have fun, and make memories. Our friend's park-model trailer sat right on the lakeshore, providing a beautiful view of all of the lake activity. In addition, there was swimming, fishing, boating, golf, shuffleboard, tennis, pickleball, badminton, mini-golf, and a small water park for younger kids, and fabulous ice cream at the Dairy Dip shop. It also offered a great chapel program with Sunday morning speakers, Sunday evening Christian concerts, Vacation Bible School, and youth group activities for the teens. It served as a different type of "happiest place on earth" getaway for our family.

It was a place where Beth knew what to expect. No surprises. It was peaceful and serene. She could be as active as she wished or sleep a lot. It was a perfect place for a getaway without all of the stimulation or expectations that caused Beth's anxiety. Sandy Pines was an incredible blessing for our family. It was something we greatly anticipated each summer.

This is how 14-year-old Beth described it to a friend of hers, as written:

> You would enjoy Sandy Pines because it is such an amazing place so peaceful yet loud at times and theres tubing and swimming and me and Callie sleep in a great loft with air beds and the sky is always so beautiful to watch at night it's so clear you can almost see every star up there and the sunsets are great and if my brother comes with Melissa then my mom, Gala, Him, and Melissa, and some other people there play CatchPhrase (a game) and watching them play is so fun because they are hilarious. I remember Melissa (Mel) last time we went my mom and her were a team and Gala

and I think Chad were a team and my mom got a word and she said "This is what moterycleists where on their heads." Melissa says "a hat!" She said a few more funny things and finally guessed it right. The word was helmet. Everyone was laughing and she just smiles.

Sandy Pines became a haven for our family, especially for Beth. Greg had a job that required weekend work, and I worked full-time during the week, so it made no sense for us to buy a trailer and lot because it was four hours away from home, and we'd hardly use it.

A few years later, Greg's job situation changed, and he didn't need to work on the weekends anymore. We bought our first trailer at Sandy Pines. After three years, we upgraded to a nearby trailer on the lake, just three lots down from my best friend, Gayla.

Beth loved Sandy Pines. It was a very therapeutic, safe getaway for her from the harsh realities of her life at home. She eagerly anticipated going there and always wanted to bring a friend. She didn't have many friends, so this was sometimes challenging. She'd plead with me, "Mom, can you find someone to come with us? Don't you have friends who have kids who would want to come?" It was heartbreaking.

I remember one time when her "friend" fell through a day or two before we left. She was incredibly upset, which meant she was incredibly angry (and difficult to live with). That caused me to be upset, too, because if Beth wasn't happy, it wasn't going to be a relaxing getaway. I remember praying, asking God to please provide a little girl who could come with us. I called several families with girls Beth's age who were interested, but the schedules didn't work. Finally, we found someone who was years older that could come, but Beth didn't care that she was older. It all worked out. *Thanks, God!*

This Sandy Pines chapter wouldn't be complete without telling this story. It happened when Beth was older, but I'll include it here since we're focusing on the summer lake house. Beth was in her late teens, hormonal and full of normal teen attitude, but her brain was also very off-kilter. Her meds needed adjustment. We had ongoing contact with the counselor and psychiatrist, but we hadn't found a medication cocktail that provided relief from Beth's serious mood swings.

This event occurred when just she and I were at Sandy Pines for the week. Greg had to return home to work. I was a bit nervous about staying there with her, away from home, considering her frame of mind, but I thought the environment might help her. After all, it was her favorite getaway place. But she struggled throughout the week with depression and anger. Nothing was right. Nothing made her happy. Her depression almost always displayed as anger.

One night, she blew up over nothing and impulsively marched out of the trailer into the dark. I didn't follow her this time. There's no way I could have kept up with her anyway. I figured that Sandy Pines (a gated community) was probably a pretty safe place—as long as she didn't walk into the lake with a plan to end it all. (She had entertained suicidal thoughts by this age.)

I prayed, earnestly begging God to protect her, to bring her back, and to give me strength and wisdom as to how to deal with the issue.

About 20 very long minutes later, my phone rang. She was calling me from about a mile away, asking me to come and get her in a soft voice because she was afraid. Sandy Pines is in the middle of nowhere in Michigan, and when it gets dark, it gets very dark. I was thankful she was afraid. I took the golf cart and picked her up.

When we got back, we had a serious talk about her depression. She was ready to express how she was feeling. She thought she would feel better at home, so I agreed to drive her back to Illinois the next day.

"I want you to understand," I explained, "that I am coming back here. I will take you home, but I'm going to turn around and come back. This is my vacation week, and I need it." She nodded as if she understood where I was coming from.

I was selfishly excited about having a few days by myself. I was just as emotionally exhausted as she was. I needed a break!

The next morning, we got up early and left about 8 a.m. It's a four-hour drive home, and she was very quiet on the trip. I had been walking on eggshells with her, as usual. When we got home, I could tell she wasn't feeling comfortable. And I didn't feel comfortable leaving and saying, "Have fun with Dad. See you Saturday!"

We talked some more, and in a very illogical turn of events, she decided she needed to stay with me and come back to Michigan. What?! Unbelievable! As I rolled my eyes (inwardly) and felt incredibly frustrated about this wasted eight-hour round-trip drive, we got back in the car and headed back to Michigan. I could not express my real emotions because that would have made the precarious situation worse. That is often the case with parents of special needs kids. We have to be the mature ones and hold our emotions inside. It's all about de-escalation in risky emotional situations. We can't blow up in frustration. If we do, the situation usually gets worse. Sometimes, much worse.

That is one of the wildest Beth stories, but we laugh about it now. There is no Mental Illness 101 instruction guide. You never know what's ahead or the "right" way to address a situation. I did what I thought was best at the time. Now we have a story we'll never forget.

We did survive the rest of the week. Things even improved. I think she saw how much I loved her and was willing to do whatever she needed, even though it was inconvenient. I had learned, by this time, to take life one day at a time, go with the flow, and not be shocked about anything. In the Bible, Matthew 6:34 encourages us not to worry about tomorrow because each day has enough trouble of its own. It's a principle I remind myself (and others) about often. ♥

8
Choosing Your Battles

By nature, I am a disciplinarian—black and white. I follow the mantra, "I am the parent, you are the kid, and you will do as I say." As the Bible says, "Children, obey your parents because you belong to the Lord, for this is the right thing to do" (Ephesians 6:1). Since God inspired that verse, it's good enough for me.

In fact, when Greg and I first started parenting counseling, the counselor said we needed to compromise in our discipline styles. At that point, Greg was the softer one, and I wanted obedience. Quick obedience, as a matter of fact. After all, this was the era of Dr. James Dobson's books, and I had read many of them. *Dare to Discipline* was a primer for me. It had worked so well for child #1, but child #2 wasn't cut out of the same fabric. Parenting 101 tells us to teach our children: "If there is disobedience, there will be consequences." Chad learned quickly. Beth—not so much.

Later on, when Beth was a teenager, Greg and I somehow switched perspectives, and he became stricter, while I loosened up. Go figure?!

We had adjusted to Beth's "diarrhea of the mouth." When we asked her to do something, we'd often be met with a barrage of oppositional words. They'd quickly come spilling out of her mouth, tumbling over each other, not making much sense sometimes. Over the years, we learned that she didn't honestly mean what she was saying or, sometimes, even know what she was saying. It seemed she had no control. She had to respond verbally to most parental requests immediately, and because of that oppositional streak, her response was often negative. Interestingly, we observed she would usually do what we asked. She just had to impulsively respond with her mouth. We learned that we needed to pay less attention to her words and focus more on her actions. This became our standard approach to her mouth because we soon learned we had bigger fish to fry. We had to choose our battles wisely.

We're not prescribing you do the same if you're in this situation. We fully believe it's not good for children to talk back to their parents. Parenting experts would concur! However, life gets messy. You do what you have to do to get through one day at a time and pray that things work out in the end.

When Beth was a preschooler, one of my friends, to whom I had poured out my heart, sent me this email:

> I thought of you the other night. I saw part of a program on 20/20 that focused on ODD. It was very interesting. They talked with a doctor who is proposing new treatments for it. Sounded like you have to compromise a lot, like a lot a lot. The family they did the story on said it worked for them. They said to other people it might seem like they're just letting the kid get his own way all the time, but it is really a series of compromises all the way, and they both end up feeling better. It gave us a new sense of admiration for you and what you're doing with Bethany.

Here was my response:

> Thank you! You're absolutely correct in saying that parents of kids with ODD feel like everyone is judging them and think their kids are brats, because that is how I feel. But I have to keep reminding myself that Beth is sick—mentally ill; and that's just the way it is. I can't compare her with a normal child, and I have to ignore others' opinions, even if they're not said out loud. I can read facial expressions!

We knew our Beth was actually a sweet girl. She was usually very quiet and shy around anyone except us because of her anxieties. When she wasn't melting down, we saw the sweet side. Often! We knew our girl, but we were not experts in dealing with the repercussions of ADHD, Asperger's, and ODD. We simply did the best we could each day and carefully chose the battles we wished to fight. We didn't have the stamina to fight them all.

We learned that some things were not as important as we once thought. Having a spotless house, preparing nutritional, homemade meals every day, participating in youth activities, and requiring she attend church with us were things that fell by the wayside.

I had tried to enroll Beth in community activities as I did with her brother, but it didn't work. She couldn't focus on the instructor in gymnastics, so she never knew what she was supposed to do. She thoroughly enjoyed running around but didn't learn much. And she didn't make any friends.

She also loved splashing around in the pool during her swimming lessons. She loved the water, but she couldn't perform the requirements to move on to the next level. Ever. To this day, she loves the water and does an amazing dog-paddle stroke. The water is therapeutic for her.

I enrolled her in a youth art class. Beth had shown an interest in art, and I thought, *Finally! Something she can excel in without having to be athletic or coordinated.* Again, she couldn't follow directions and interact with the other kids, even though we signed up for the class with her neighborhood friend. I thought that might help.

So, I gave up on those types of group activities. It was no use beating my head against the wall again and again. Those were battles we didn't need to fight.

When Beth was nine or ten, she begged to get her ears pierced. I thought she was too young, but she really didn't have a lot of things to look forward to, and she was excited about this possibility. I relented, and off we marched to Claire's at the mall. They had a special piercing gun they used, with the caveat that you purchase their starter earrings.

Beth was very excited and carefully picked out the earrings she wanted. Even though she was petrified, she really wanted pierced ears. She climbed up on the chair and let the young girl pierce her left ear. Then she decided that hurt a lot, and she didn't want the other ear pierced.

Maralee Parker

We might have just gone home if I had the insight then that I do now. This wasn't a huge battle I needed to fight, and it would be funny down the road. She would probably decide, on her own, that she needed the other ear pierced, and we'd go back and finish the job. Or, she'd let it grow back, and that would be the end of the story.

But at that time, I felt she could not be lopsided, and she needed to finish what she had started. The worker told her she could rest a little, and then we'd do the other one. So, Beth walked around the store, FAR away from me. I knew my girl and knew I had to be wise in dealing with this. I couldn't tell her what to do. I had to suggest. I had to sound warm and loving and not confrontational. Although I was thinking, *Get over there and sit down! Of course, you're going to get the other ear pierced, silly. You can't go around with just one pierced ear.*

I had been down this road many, many times. I knew what I needed to do, but I never knew how it would end. The store was getting ready to close. That meant more stress for Beth. She had to make up her mind, and she had to do it quickly. I bit my lip, not saying anything that might set her off, but basically repeating softly what the clerk said, "We need to finish up so the store can close, honey."

Eventually, she did it. (Whew!) We went home with not one but two pierced ears.

Of course, she didn't follow through and let them grow back together, and two years later, we were back again. *Sigh.* Never a dull moment.

Another memorable Beth story involved a neighborhood cat. By this time, Beth was 13 or so and was staying home alone after school while I worked three miles away. She enjoyed riding her bike around the neighborhood, and on this particular day, she saw a cat lying near a church building. She rode home and called me.

"Mom, I found a cat by the church. It's lying down in the corner and looks like it's hungry. Can I bring it home?"

"No, Beth. We already have three cats. We don't need another one."

"But it looks like it doesn't have a home. And it's hungry."

"No, Beth."

"Well, can I at least take some food over there for it?"

(Here's where the compromise comes in.) "Fine. Take a little bit of our cat food over and a little water. But leave the cat there!"

A little later, I'm telling my friends at work about the cat story and kind of chuckling about it when I get another phone call.

"Mom, I took some food to that cat, and it bit me!"

I wasn't chuckling anymore. I jumped up, explained the situation to my boss, and headed home. We washed her bite, put some antibiotic lotion on it and a Band-Aid. Then I told her to take me to the cat. I was worried this cat might have rabies!

We drove over to the church, and she showed me where she found the cat. Fortunately, the cat was still there. Unfortunately, the cat was dead! That's right. The cat was dead.

My daughter had just been bitten by a cat, which then died. I wasn't sure what to do, but I was worried. I called the nonemergency police number, and a squad car came out and removed the dead cat. He told us we should get Beth checked out at the ER, so we did. When we arrived and told the story, I remember the nurse asking, "So, let me be sure I have this right. The cat bit you, and then the cat died?" She was trying to joke around a little.

Beth got a shot of something that would help her fight any germs the cat may have had, and they bandaged her up and sent her home. Later, we learned that the police had sent the cat for a rabies test, and it was negative.

What a relief! That was quite an eventful afternoon. I'm glad I didn't agree to let her bring the cat home, but I probably should have stuck to my guns and told her to leave it alone. Knowing her, I doubt she would have listened to me, especially since I was at work.

All's well that ends well. Right?

We also decided to compromise about pets. I grew up on a farm, and along with chickens, pigs, cows, and barn cats, we always had a dog. I've always loved animals. And it's a good thing.

Greg and I had our first dog, Brutus (all 10 pounds of him), for 10 years until he died. Beth was very young at that time. We also had a cat named Stormie. She was all black and a sweetheart. We added two more cats and enjoyed them for many years. Two of them passed, and that's when Beth started begging for a dog.

"Pleeeeeeeease, Mom?" She kept at it for months until I weakened. It didn't take that much begging, truth be told, because I am truly a dog lover, but I also worked full-time. I explained to Beth that no one would be home during the day to care for a puppy. Cats were much more independent and easier, and that's why we had cats.

Eventually, I gave in (and I was secretly excited!). We went to a breeder, and Beth picked out a darling little black Pomeranian puppy. We brainstormed together and settled on the name Romeo. We were a happy family with one cat and one dog—temporarily.

It didn't take long before Beth realized Romeo was attached to me, followed me everywhere, and didn't want much to do with anyone else.

"Mom, I want a dog of my own. I want a dog that will be my dog."

I gently told her that dogs get to choose who they want as their master, and even if we got another dog, it didn't mean the dog would choose her.

At this time, Beth was not stable. She was a teenager, and life was very hard. I looked for things to make her smile, keep her happy, and give her a purpose to get up in the morning. Her life was different from most kids because she had only one friend and couldn't participate in typical kid activities because of her anxiety and autism. She just sat at home and became more and more depressed.

One day, as was our tradition, we stopped at a pet store for fun. Usually, it cheered her up just to see the pets. But this day, she fell in love with a dachshund puppy. Greg and I had already talked about getting a second dog, so I thought he would be on board with moving ahead because he realized, as I did, that we needed to find something that would encourage Beth. (I did make a quick call to confirm with him.) We ended up taking that adorable little puppy home. We named her Juliet to go along with Romeo. (I'm no longer a fan of pet stores, and I'd go directly to a breeder or a dog rescue organization if I could go back in time.)

Beth enjoyed Juliet at first, but she became disillusioned after a week or so. Dachshunds aren't typical dogs who worship you. They can be independent and obstinate. They were bred to hunt badgers, so they had to be gutsy to get that critter. Often, they don't run to you. In fact, when we would call Juliet, she went the opposite way. She was so stubborn!

Beth decided this wasn't the dog for her. I wanted to scream. I had tried so hard to help her find something to make her happy, and evidently, this expensive dog was not it. I thought I could sell the puppy and recover some of our money, and I did have someone interested, but I decided I could not sell this adorable puppy! I had fallen in love with her. Greg felt the same way, although he'd deny it if you asked him. We now had one cat and two dogs.

But, Beth still didn't have "her" dog to cuddle and love. We did some research this time on dog temperaments. She ended up picking a toy American Eskimo dog. We drove four hours to pick her up from the breeder. Now we had three small, yappy dogs in our house (and two were puppies).

Gracie has been Beth's dog for 12 years now. When we brought her home, I was very careful with Gracie. I didn't look at her or pet her. I gave Gracie no attention (although I did feed her along with the other two). And wonder of wonders, Gracie bonded with Beth. Beth had herself a dog! Finally.

Before the era of three dogs, we went through many pets. I didn't necessarily want any of these pets in my house, but again, I was choosing my battles, and I wasn't going to fight about a pet who might give Beth some joy and purpose. So, over the years, we've had cats, dogs, fish, mice and rats, gerbils and hamsters, guinea pigs, rabbits, a chinchilla, ferrets, snakes, a pony and a horse.

We had a zoo! We had one kind of pet at a time (besides the cats/dogs). If Beth couldn't handle the pet after a while, we'd find a new home for it. Alyssa, her animal-loving friend, took several of them. I was so very thankful for her. We also have a small, family-owned pet store nearby that rehomes pets. They took several off of our hands, including the rats and snakes. I was very thankful for that store!

It bothers me to say this happened pretty often. She would be very excited about getting a particular pet, but then, she emotionally couldn't handle the care of it. If she was a *normal* kid, I wouldn't have let her return the pet or give it to someone else. Once she had committed to the pet, I would teach her responsibility. But she wasn't normal.

For example, when Chad was a kid, he wanted to take piano lessons. He begged. I agreed but told him he had to commit for a year, even if he didn't like it after he started. He agreed and took lessons—for one year. He was very happy to finish that year.

Maralee Parker

Chad wanted to be a newspaper carrier, and I said the same thing. "This is your job. I will not be folding the papers or helping you. If you want to do it, you can, but you have to do all the work, and you have to commit to it." This is the way I wanted to parent and build responsibility. It worked with Chad, but my usual parenting techniques didn't work the same way with Beth.

Although Greg doesn't think so, we have a funny pet story concerning one of Beth's pets. Greg sometimes falls asleep in a chair in the living room, and I let him sleep when I go to our bedroom. One night, he stormed into our room, woke me up and said, "Some little furry thing was just climbing up my leg!"

I jumped up and woke Beth. One of her rats had escaped the cage and was having an exciting trip around the house in the middle of the night—and ended up crawling inside one of Greg's pant legs. I chuckle as I recall it—because it happened to him. Neighbors two blocks away would have heard me scream if I had been the recipient of the surprise midnight rodent visit.

Pets can (usually) be incredibly therapeutic in the life of a mentally ill person or the life of any person. As I'm writing this, COVID-19 is spreading worldwide, and we're required to stay home much more than usual. What makes me happy? My two dogs. They snuggle with me every chance they get. I love having their warm, furry little bodies curled up in my lap. When the world is sad, my fur babies' unconditional love makes me smile.

Here's another example of choosing your battles from when Beth was in high school.

Beth wanted to buy a prom dress. She is unable to shop for a prom dress a month before prom like most girls. She needs to do it five months before prom so she can stop worrying about it. She begged to go shopping for weeks, and I eventually gave in. I knew her well enough to know I could suffer for months, listening to her anxiety, or just buy the dress now.

We went to a bridal store, and she found one within my budget she liked, but she wasn't positive it was "the" dress. She wanted to look in one other store at the mall. We went there, and she found one there she really liked, too.

Now we had a dilemma. Normal kids would simply make a decision, even though it might be hard. But Beth became more agitated and angrier as I gently encouraged her to decide. Her anxiety took over, and she couldn't decide. Nor could she leave the store. She was stuck. Then she started running away from me—a typical response when she became overwhelmed.

This was a big store in a huge enclosed mall. I gave her space (I have learned) but kept an eye on her as she walked around looking at things, glaring at me. I did not want to lose sight of her. I prayed, as usual.

This went on for an hour or so, which seemed like an eternity. She could not leave the store. Nor could she make a decision.

God answered my prayer. He gave me wisdom. What I said next to Beth was way outside of my normal way of thinking (and I knew Greg probably wouldn't be too excited about my "wisdom").

"Beth, since you can't make up your mind between the two dresses, how about this idea. I will buy both dresses—if you agree to wear one this year and the other one next year. We will not be buying another dress next year."

That solved the battle. She calmed down, and we bought the dress. We then went back to the other store and bought that dress. We came home with two dresses. I pulled Greg aside, and while batting my eyes, I told him the whole challenging story. I believe there was some eye-rolling on his part, but he eventually understood.

Beth kept her part of the bargain. She had her prom dress ready for this year, and she had her prom dress ready for the next year, which she did indeed wear. She didn't need to worry about it anymore.

Remember earlier when I described what I call "diarrhea of the mouth?" When she was a teen and became angry, all kinds of nasty words would come pouring out of her mouth. She screamed profanities that, as my husband says, "would make a longshoreman blush." Most of them were aimed at me. She rarely screamed at her dad. I think she was afraid of him at the time, not because of anything he had done, but because he has a scary voice and can be very intimidating. She was actually a sweet, shy girl with a sick brain, and she didn't like the way he talked when he was upset with her. How ironic is that?

It does seem that mothers often get the brunt of their challenging kids' anger. I've heard story after story where the mom gets screamed at, physically attacked, and blamed for everything. I think it's because kids know their moms usually have abundant unconditional love for them. They trust they can let all their raging emotion out on this person, and she will still love them. It's a hard job for moms.

Her anger was unleashed on me regularly, mostly through her abusive choice of words, but sometimes nearby objects were thrown. Occasionally, I'd get shoved. We had told her that if she physically assaulted her father or me, we would call the police. I think that helped her control herself to some extent, even in the midst of extreme rage. She hated and feared the police.

I remember one story that I'm somewhat embarrassed to share, but here goes. When I was working full-time, I'd often come home, prepare dinner, clean up, and retreat to our bedroom to catch up on a recorded TV show. It was "me time," when I could relax and have a little peace and quiet. At least, that was the goal.

Beth had a habit of coming in with her latest problem and going on and on about it. The psychological term for it is "perseveration." Sometimes the topic of her obsession would last for weeks or months. She'd start talking and couldn't seem to stop. She would get angry about whatever her concern was, often blaming me. She'd start using profanity and just stand there being obnoxious but also seemingly unable to move physically from her spot. One night something clicked in my brain (perhaps similar to Towanda in *Fried Green Tomatoes*), and I decided I'd turn it around and give it right back to her. I knew it would elicit a response. I started yelling, using some of the choice words she used (which I never used; nor did I normally yell), and wonder of wonders, that shut her up! She was dumbfounded and wondered what had happened to her mother. It got her attention. It worked, and she left my room. Later, when we talked it out, she told me, "Mothers shouldn't be using those words." (Go ahead, laugh! I did!)

Choose your battles wisely. This is very true with neurotypical kids, but the "normal" rules often need to be thrown out the window when raising a child with mental illness. You, and only you, have to make the difficult decisions about what is best for your child and what is best for you. You may need to ignore comments family and friends throw at you. They don't live your life. They aren't facing constant rages and physical attacks. They don't walk on eggshells every day, hoping to avoid another huge meltdown. They just don't get it because, as Beth said earlier, "They aren't *me*." How could we expect them to understand what they haven't experienced?

We didn't know it then, but there were much bigger battles ahead for us. ♥

9

Pretending to be Normal

It was time for middle school. Kids at this age are entering puberty, with all the physical and emotional challenges it brings. Parents of normal kids often dread those years. It's such a period of change and adjustment for everyone.

Beth wasn't up for it. Her life became even more challenging. Back in fifth grade, she had qualified for an IEP (Individual Education Plan), so we had regular meetings with her teacher and other professionals at her school who had worked with her for several years already. At her last IEP meeting in sixth grade, we all sat around the table wondering what to do with Beth for middle school. What would be best for her? Where could she fit in and feel comfortable—and be successful?

Truth be told, she didn't fit anywhere. After kicking around possibilities, the educational team concluded the self-contained BD (behavior disorder) class was the best option. She wouldn't have to navigate the noise and stress of changing classrooms. She'd stay in the same room for most of the day, with a small number of students. The decision was made. I didn't fully understand what a BD class was, so I didn't have much input at that point. I trusted the "experts."

Middle school is very different from elementary school. Our middle school tried to help the transition by having an open house for incoming seventh-graders prior to the first day of school. I knew Beth needed to attend it. She would need all of the transition help she could get to have a successful year. She was scared to death of middle school, as many kids are. Multiply that anxiety by 10 for Beth.

She and I attended the open house. Her anxiety caused her to be angry and agitated the entire time. I wanted her to learn where the restrooms were and how to get to her classroom, at the very least. As we walked to her room, she became angrier and angrier. This was from her anxiety cresting. On our way, we saw a girl and her parents from our church in the hallway. My hope rose, thinking this was someone Beth would recognize, although she didn't know her well. I stopped to say hi, but Beth had no interest in chit-chat. She wanted to get out of there immediately. I knew nothing productive would happen at that point, so we left. She was angry the rest of the night. *Oh, yeah. Seventh grade is going to be a lot of fun.*

I sent a letter to her new teacher, paving the way for Beth, as I did each year. I added a note about P.E. "Beth is very worried about P.E. She hates it and has repeatedly said she 'doesn't understand what she is supposed to do.' It makes her feel stupid, and she thinks no one likes her because she 'can't do anything,' she says. I am asking the school to be aware of this need and give extra support so it doesn't become a major problem. I hope she'll be able to participate at least minimally, but I want you and the P.E. teacher to be aware of her challenges."

I was trying to help smooth the way, but I also knew that this would be a bumpy year no matter what I did. But I had no idea how bumpy.

I drove her there the first day, of course. I walked with her up to the BD room and introduced her to the teacher. I then learned there were 10 boys in the classroom—and Beth. The teacher was nice enough, but he was a man. Beth didn't like men. She always connected much better with women, especially young women. This was not a good omen.

Fortunately, a cute, young female was doing her student teaching in that classroom. Beth immediately connected with her. The first couple of months of school were very challenging, but I was able to get her to school most of the time because "Miss Owens" was there. Miss Owens was kind to Beth. I thanked God for Miss Owens.

However, Miss Owens completed her internship after the first quarter, and school became exceedingly more difficult for Beth at that time. It was her and the boys.

She had a hard time riding the bus. She had a hard time when she got to school. She had a hard time in P.E. (required). She had a hard

Maralee Parker

time—period. I had a hard time getting her to attend school every day. Her attendance record was not good. It was definitely a hard time!

Here's a letter I gave Beth in December of that year, trying to encourage her. She never listened when I spoke to her. She got angry, so I chose to write.

> Dear Daniel's girl, [She loved fantasy and called herself this—it was the Daniel Radcliffe obsession era.]
>
> Hi. It's a letter. A letter from Mom!
>
> I love to write, and you hate to listen, so I thought I would drop you a line. That way you don't have to listen. ☺
>
> Today, I'm proud of you for going to school and riding the bus home. I hope the reading teacher understands you better now and that P.E. is going to be easier for you now that you have someone to help you out a bit there.
>
> We'll keep trying to be on your side, Beth. We want to help you with the problems you might have in school. But you need to do your part, too. Right now, as Dad and I go off to our jobs every day, you need to go off to your job, which, right now, is school. You need to be able to ride the bus—either a little one with hardly any kids or a big one with your friends. Every day. Dad or I can't pick you up because our bosses don't like that!
>
> I'm happy you like Harry Potter. It's fun. More fun than Ronin Warriors. I promise I will read the book after Dad is finished. ☺
>
> We love you!
> Mom and Dad

It was around this time Beth started having physical problems with her bladder. I took her to the doctor, to a pediatric urologist, and to a regular urologist. There was testing, with no medical problems discovered. Yet she did have physical problems, and she had learned to sit on a blanket for hours, in a certain way, to get relief from the pain. It may have been psychological, but it was evidenced physically. That went off and on for several years.

When her "problem" was bothering her, I couldn't get her to school. She had missed at least 30% of school days by the time Christmas arrived. Her grades were headed downhill. We had ongoing meetings with the counseling staff and others at the school, trying to find a way to make things work.

Here's an excerpt from an email I sent to a friend concerning this school-phobia period:

I had a really rough morning with Beth today...she had been sick all week (kidney infection) and basically refused to go to school today. I knew she was fine and was ready to go back to school. And I knew I had to WIN *this* battle. I let go of many, but this was one I knew I had to fight for. Otherwise, I'd hear "sick excuses" whenever she didn't want to go to school. So, I insisted that, yes, she was going to school. It was a war. Screaming on her side, encouragement to "hurry up" on my side. The wooden spoon appeared. I really don't use it anymore, but it does usually get results when I bring it out. I tried reasoning, threats, encouragement. I went out to the car to wait for her to come out. This often works, as it gives her space and a choice as to when she will come out, without standing right in her face, which definitely doesn't work with her. I pray when I'm waiting in the car. For strength. Wisdom. Patience. I had to go back in the house THREE times this morning. School starts at 8 a.m. I eventually got her there at 8:30. She had hit me once, kicked me once, and swore a boatload at me, but I DID get her there. I told her I was calling the school to come and get her if she didn't come out (and I would, and they would). She HATED that idea. That's what got her to come out eventually.

Maralee Parker

When we got to school, the moment she stepped inside, she was a different person. Quiet. Shy. Cooperative. Smiles at the school secretary, and I'm wondering, "WHO IS THIS CHILD?" She even smiled at me because I made a mistake with her teacher's name and then made a joke of it. Anyway, I sensed things were moving forward in a more positive way.

I left, fighting back tears. I usually stay tough through these "Beth meltdowns," but when they are over, I sometimes collapse emotionally. When I shared my morning with two friends at work, I cried both times. It's so stressful. I can tell when I am at my breaking point with the stress, when I am constantly on the verge of tears.

When I got home after work, I tried to talk about the morning with her, but she was over it. She started screaming again, making no sense. I gave up. I didn't have the energy to make it a learning opportunity. Sigh.

I'll never forget the IEP meeting that year when a young, single, male counselor (with no children) accused us of letting her manipulate us. He suggested that, perhaps, discipline was the problem. We needed to discipline her more. Being a Christian woman, I refrained from punching him, not to say I didn't want to!

I'll forever be grateful for Beth's psychiatrist (who happened to be a consulting psychiatrist for our school district), who agreed to a teleconference during an IEP meeting. In his professional way, he provided facts to explain some of Beth's deficits and challenges. That helped immensely.

Remember Brenda from fifth grade? The collaborative interventionist who called to yell at me for not making Beth do her homework? She had come full circle by this time, and she attended the IEP meetings with us to provide other supportive professional information because she had worked so closely with Beth. Plus, Brenda knew the ins and outs of IEP meetings. She brought along her portable keyboard and typed the conversations as they occurred. We were so grateful! I so appreciated her help and her willingness to support us. She honestly had Beth's best interests in mind.

Things went from bad to worse in the second semester of seventh grade. It was a struggle every day to get Beth to school. By this time, I had changed my work schedule and agreed to drive her to school every morning (one less stressor for her). I remember trying to be casual to avoid adding more stress to the situation. I'd say, "Okay, honey, finish getting ready. I'll be waiting in the car for you."

Then, I'd wait, pray, and sometimes cry. I never let Beth know I had been crying if she did come out and slide in next to me. On the days I couldn't get her to the car, I felt like a failure. I couldn't even get my child to school!

But always—God is good. Twila Paris, a well-known Christian singer at the time, had a hit, "God Is in Control." I heard it play often as I sat in the car with the radio on, waiting. God was reminding me that He was with me, even if He didn't immediately fix the situation. He, the creator of the universe, was in control, even of this Beth situation. I needed to trust Him.

By now, she was missing more days than she attended. The school began to realize the extent of our problem. A female school counselor and I met, discussing why it was so hard to get Beth to school. In desperation, I invited her to come to our home and see what she could do. I said, "You're welcome to come and give it a try yourself if you'd like!" (Perhaps with just a little bit of attitude.)

To my amazement, she did. I think it was a February morning when she pulled into our driveway. I told Beth she was coming, and Beth, in her immature, child-like way, was a little excited that "Miss Johnson" was coming to our house. When the counselor came in, Beth was sitting there in her pajamas. Miss Johnson made some small talk with her, which Beth enjoyed. Then the atmosphere changed when the counselor said, "Well, it's time to get ready for school. Go get dressed, Beth."

Beth slumped down, shook her head a little, and stopped talking. The counselor explained that it was the law that kids needed to go to school. That didn't faze Beth. Miss Johnson continued prodding her, encouraging her, threatening her. Finally, she said that she would have to call the truant officer at the police station and have the officer come to take Beth to school.

I know this was elevating Beth's anxiety big-time. (It was elevating my anxiety big-time.) Beth just sat in the chair. The counselor explained privately to me that the school officer was in "plain clothes" that day, and she felt Beth needed to see an officer in uniform to provide an authoritative appearance. So, in a few minutes, a police car with two officers showed up to convince Beth she needed to go to school. By this time, Beth had locked herself in the bathroom, and I was crying in the kitchen. *Seriously? Was this necessary?* I grabbed the bathroom key. I tried to give the officer a quick update on Beth's situation before I unlocked the door. He appeared clueless.

I had tried to explain Beth's severe anxiety and anger issues all along, but evidently, the school had to follow protocol. The officers did not convince Beth to get dressed and eventually left, as did the counselor. What a nightmare!

This was not a truancy problem; this was a mental illness problem.

That was one of the worst days of my life. Thank God we can't see what's ahead, as there would be more of those days coming.

My husband had sent letters to the school concerning Beth's needs and the district's lack of progress in meeting them throughout the year, all certified, requiring signatures for delivery. We were prepared to take the school to court, along with the help of an organization specializing in these types of cases, to provide an appropriate education for Beth, which was the law. And the school knew it.

At the next IEP meeting, the school officials began to cooperate more and see our side of the story. Beth was failing all classes, and by March, wasn't attending school at all. The school listened to us and realized Beth would not be successful in a public school setting. Then a miracle occurred. They actually invited us to visit and observe three other special education settings in their district, which we did. We were shocked that they also said we could look at private schools if the district's options didn't look promising in meeting Beth's needs.

We were open-minded and visited two learning disorder classes and another very small behavior disorder class in different locations in the large school district. We didn't feel any of them would be a successful fit. So, we broadened our visits to include private, special education schools. We visited one that specialized in autism. It was an hour away (a two-hour round trip bus ride each day), but I thought it would be perfect because they would understand Beth's needs. But by the time we applied there, they were full for the fall. I was very disappointed.

We visited another one that was only 30 minutes from home and decided we would move forward with this school. It seemed God opened the door there and closed it for the one I had preferred (for autistic kids). Her public school district agreed with our decision, which was amazing since it would cost them many thousands of dollars to send a student there for the year. After we filled out the necessary paperwork, Beth was accepted. She would begin there in the fall. We were somewhat concerned because many types of disabilities were represented at this school. Many of the kids didn't look "normal" because of their disabilities. We weren't sure how Beth would react. Beth looked normal. Her problems were mental and developmental. Sometimes that was a blessing, and sometimes not, because people expected her to respond in a normal way and were confused when she didn't.

We were thankful for a new chapter. It gave a new ray of hope for the fall. All we could do was encourage Beth and do our best to help her be successful at her new school. ♥

10

The Terrible, Horrible, No Good, Very Bad Day

We had a plan. Everything's better when there's a plan, right? We had just endured an awful seventh-grade year with Beth (I often call it "the year from hell"), but we now had a plan! We were all anticipating that the new school was going to work out. But before the school year started, we had summer to relax and enjoy our lake house. At least, that was the plan.

By this time, Beth was 14. It's a challenging time for most parents, as their children are physically sprouting and experiencing hormonal changes but still have immature brains. It's challenging for the kids, too.

I'll never forget the day that we leveled up with Beth, but I don't mean that in a positive way. Up to this point, we were managing, although life was exhausting and difficult for everyone in our family, including her. But on this day, in June 2001, things were going to get much more serious.

I came home from work and found a note, in Beth's child-like printing, telling me she and her friend had decided to run away. She told me not to look for them. She didn't want to live with us anymore. They were going to go live by themselves "somewhere."

After reading that note from her and breathing again, I called Greg, Chad, and his fiancée, Melissa. Soon we were out in our cars, driving the neighborhood, searching for them. Greg covered home base in case she came back while the rest of us were out.

I didn't even know her friend's last name. I had no way to alert her parents. This wasn't a close friend. She had only been to our house briefly once or twice before. I didn't know where she lived.

I was so scared! Beth was a very naïve 13-year-old girl, and it was starting to get dark. Where was she? I begged God to keep her safe. I tried to use my left-brained, logical mind (but I'm more of a right-brained person) to think where they might have gone. For some reason (perhaps the Holy Spirit's leading), I had a gut instinct to check the Walgreens store near our house. It was within walking distance, and was one of Beth's favorite places. I drove there and ran in, just in time to see them at the checkout counter! The minute they saw me, they left everything and ran out the front door and off into the dark. Before I had walked in, the clerk had just alerted the manager as they were trying to use my credit card, and she was suspicious. They were trying to buy hair dye (to change their appearance) and some food and drinks.

There was no way I would catch them, so I got in my car and made the split-second decision to call the police. I didn't want to but knew I had to. I needed their help. Who thought it would ever come to this—needing to bring in law enforcement to control our 14-year-old daughter? It wasn't just a private Parker family situation any longer.

Chad, Melissa, and I continued to scour the neighborhood, and now police cars were joining us. I prayed as my eyes darted up and down streets. Finally, Chad called me and said the police had spotted them in a nearby park and apprehended them. Later, we learned they had planned to walk down the railroad tracks and "catch a train." Oh, my sweet, naïve baby girl!

The officers brought them to the police station. They had separated them and handled them individually, so I never saw the other girl, although I knew who she was.

When I drove up, Beth was sitting on the ground, under a streetlamp in front of the police station, arms tightly folded, scowling. I could tell she was furious. There were a couple of police officers "guarding" her. Yes, this was my "sweet, shy" daughter. Now what? I knew it wouldn't be good to bring her home. She was in a fighting mood, not stable, and would probably run again. They suggested the local hospital to help her calm down. The hospital had a behavioral health floor, if needed.

It all felt surreal. I had no idea what else to do, so I agreed, and they proceeded to escort Beth to the back seat of the squad. I met them at the hospital. Before they got Beth into the ER, something set her off, and she bit one of the officers! I'm so very thankful they didn't press charges on this kid—this girl who seemed to be in a very bad place. Fight or flight? She was doing both, literally and figuratively, on this very bad day. I'm so thankful they realized this was the result of mental illness, not teenage rebellion.

She was very agitated, so the hospital staff wanted to give her something to help her calm down. She flat out refused to see me. She was mad at the world at this point. This wasn't a typical Beth scenario. She was an angry kid, for sure, but she was also extremely shy and didn't ever want to be the center of attention. She very rarely acted out in public. She saved it all for home. All of the signs pointed to something being very wrong.

They gave her Haldol, which knocked her out for a whole day.

I sat in the waiting room of that ER, trying to comprehend what had just happened. Greg met me there, and I brought him up to speed, then I knew I needed to get in touch with her psychiatrist to get his advice. He recommended transferring her to a nearby behavioral hospital that specialized in treating children and teens. (He was also on staff there and could treat Beth, which would be very helpful.) It was about 30 minutes away. So around 1 a.m., I followed Beth, who was in a deep sleep on a gurney, as she was transported into an ambulance and driven to this new hospital. As Greg drove, I sat, speechless. I was numb. Was this really happening?

The intake interview was long and daunting at the behavioral hospital. They require so much information. My brain wasn't working well after the traumatic events of the day (and night). After an hour or more of providing information, they said we could leave. Walking away, I felt like we were deserting her.

She was in that hospital for two weeks. They stopped all meds and started "fresh" to test the efficacy of a new medicine cocktail. Obviously, what she was on was not working. They provided individual and group counseling. She could have very few of her possessions there—and, of course, nothing that could aid in a suicide attempt. They insisted on daily showers and other requirements. It was very structured, which can sometimes be beneficial and provide security for a mentally-ill person.

I was concerned about the influence of the other girls there. She was obviously on an all-girls floor, with locked doors and highly authoritative staff everywhere (imagine drill sergeant stereotype). Many of the girls were wards of the state, without parents or with parents who couldn't properly care for them. Here was our sweet, naïve 14-year-old, who had the maturity of maybe an 8-year-old, mixed in with some very street-wise kids. I prayed—without ceasing!

Those two weeks were a blessed relief for Greg and me in some ways. We knew where Beth was and that she was being cared for. We didn't need to hear profanity screamed at us on a daily basis. We didn't need to walk on eggshells. We could do what we wanted, when we wanted, and sleep all night, peacefully. We felt a little guilty feeling as we did, but we needed that reprieve after so much stress for so long. I've since learned it's a common response from parents in this type of situation.

The hospital allowed her to call during "phone hour." She suddenly had a change of heart on her first day there and wanted to talk to me. Imagine that! She talked to me as if there had never been a huge incident the day before (so typical of her). She asked me if I could come and visit her during visiting time and bring her favorite stuffed animal. *Sigh.* This was the story of my life! She acted as if this wasn't a big deal while we were left reeling from it.

Greg and I did visit. It was very different from a typical hospital. If I recall, we couldn't bring in my purse, and anything we did bring in for the patient had to be examined. The only place to visit was in a small lobby waiting room, where a few others were also visiting. Sadly, there wasn't a need for a huge meeting area because many of the girls didn't have family, so they never had visitors.

I'll never forget the scene that first day when it was time for us to leave. It will be imprinted on my brain and forever in my heart. Beth didn't want us to go and started crying and then sobbing while desperately holding on to me. Greg and I stood up and started walking toward the elevator, gently telling her visiting time was over and that we had to go. We assured her we'd come again tomorrow, but she kept clinging to me, sobbing and pleading, "Mom! Mom, please don't leave me here!" (This is the girl who doesn't want to be the center of attention. She was desperate.)

A couple of large, muscular men were then summoned. They quickly appeared and pulled her away as gently as they could. They were kind but were there for a purpose. I'm sure that frightened her even more. By this time, she was on the floor, clinging to my ankles as they were trying to grab her hands. I will never forget that heartrending day. I was crying too.

Things were better after Beth was released from the hospital. She was incredibly happy to be back home, yet transitions were always hard for her, so it took a day or two for her to settle back into her "normal."

But it didn't take long before the rages and moods came back, although the new medicine seemed to be taking some of the edge off. We were grateful for any improvement. Onward to "enjoying" summer and looking forward to the new school in the fall. ♥

Reading, Writing,
and Teenage Boys

The long-awaited day came. It was the long-dreaded day, as far as Beth was concerned. This was not going to be an easy day—for anyone. It was time to go to the new school.

We had tried to casually play it up, explaining this school was smaller, and the teachers understood kids with disabilities. The class she was assigned to had only eight or nine students, many of who were taught individually at their level of understanding. Yet, it was a very challenging day, as expected.

Here's an email that I sent to a friend about that first day of school:

> Yesterday was Beth's first day at Heritage, and it was awful. Last night was also awful, as she complained about her day. She hates the school. She doesn't want to be with "retards," as she says. It's true that the kids in her class are academically below her level, and some do look a bit "off." I think they placed her in the wrong class. She needs to be in the next class up. She went on and on last night about how she WASN'T going, and it was the WRONG place, and we were AWFUL parents. I didn't know if we were going to get her to school today or not...praying through it all...but she just got on the bus. Now there's sweet peace and quiet at home. Poor Chilly

(her cat) gets a few hours of freedom, too. I feel sorry for him as she usually controls him, making him stay in her room all the time.

I have doubts as to whether Heritage is going to work. I don't know WHAT is going to work!?! She wants to be home-schooled. I can't do that. I work full time. She doesn't listen to me. I can't get five words out in a row before she interrupts me. It would never work in a million years! She also needs outside influence, or she gets too depressed...nothing worth living for when you're stuck in a box day after day, you know? Same old every day, looking at the four walls. She needs friends. It's so hard to find a friend she wants and can be a friend to...she told me this morning the kids at Heritage are disabled, and there's "nothing wrong with her." I started to gently remind her of some of her challenges, then she gets mad at me and starts screaming/swearing at me. She just loves the F-bomb. UGH. She is soooo difficult and challenging and unique. And it's just so hard on me, especially. Greg stays quiet for most of it, not being as intuitive as I, and not knowing exactly how to comment without causing another eruption. I stay strong, stay strong, stay strong as Beth goes on and on and on. I mostly listen with an occasional comment. Then when I'm alone—I sob! It's so emotionally hard! Beth is so volatile emotionally. She can go from smiling and laughing and talking with me to swearing and stomping off and sometimes even swatting me (3x last night) to smiling and laughing and talking again—all within a few minutes. Again and again this repeats. That dysfunctional emotional roller coaster is so hard on "normal" people. It's hard to keep up.

So that's how it's going with Beth. She has four more days of evaluation, then we have an intake meeting at Heritage. I don't know if I'm going to get her there four more days. I don't know what else to do either. She talks about wanting to go back to her middle school with an aide with her. Then we'd have the lunch issue, the noise issue, the bus issue, the P.E. issue, the overwhelming sensory environment again, but with "normal" kids around. We thought a smaller setting would be so much better for her, and I think it is. But there are drawbacks everywhere, it seems.

She talked last night about how she LIKED the hospital! (Insert eye roll here.) I could tell she did like parts of it, which is kind of scary. It was safe, very predictable, and she was locked up with other girls her age. She had FRIENDS, so to speak!

Life is just so difficult with Beth. Thanks for your continued prayers.

The first couple of days of this new private school were difficult, just as we expected. We knew by now that the first few days of anything was difficult for her. Change and transition were always very hard. Her anxiety reigned supreme in these situations, preventing her from functioning. That is why we moved her to this school to have less anxiety. It would take time, and we all needed the patience to give it time to work.

Here is the memo I sent to the principal and teacher of the new school, the district placement coordinator from the public school, our family therapist, and Beth's psychiatrist.

Beth's Heritage experience thus far (after six days of school).

Greetings! Beth's been at Heritage for six out of eight school days thus far. She started on Aug. 28 and missed Sept. 3 and 4, saying her "problem" (a mysterious urinary-related problem, perhaps caused by anxiety) was bothering her. Every single morning is a major battle to get her to school. She seems very unhappy. She seems very anxious. She seems very angry. Thus far, it doesn't seem to be working at Heritage. I didn't want to have to do this so soon, but I had to drive her there this morning. Emotionally, she couldn't get on the bus and was almost hysterical by the time I sent it away. I was just so relieved I could still get her to school, even if I did have to drive her (and miss a meeting at work).

She called me at work when she got home today very angry about the school day, and of course, saying she's not going tomorrow. These seem to be her biggest complaints:

1. She "doesn't belong in a school like that." She "is smart; they are not." She wants to "be cool and dress cool; they do not care." She complains about the school being too gentle, which I think is a hoot! (That's exactly what she needs. She just doesn't know it.)

2. P.E. and the P.E. teacher cause her great distress. Beth says he expects a lot, but P.E. has always been a major stressor for her. The idea of any organized game or activity causes her a great deal of anxiety. If the teacher reprimands her in any way, she's done. As she said tonight to me, she is "extremely sensitive" about that, and that is an understatement. She has never been able to accept criticism without totally overreacting.

3. Is there any way she could be around some other girls? Even if she could go somewhere else for one class? That might help. She really needs girlfriends. There is only one girl (Sarah) in her G36 classroom, and I did hear a positive comment tonight about her. (She had given Sarah her phone number.) She needs more friends to help her want to come to school, especially young teens. She needs to feel there's a sense of "coolness" there at Heritage through other girls who are concerned about teenage girl things.

4. Cindy had asked that she not bring personal things to class, and I can understand that they might be distracting. Unfortunately, Beth needs to have a familiar thing or two, usually a picture or a book, to feel comfortable. She often takes pictures of her current obsession, Daniel Radcliffe (Harry Potter actor), with her wherever she goes, even sometimes from room to room at home, at the movie theater, and in the car. She spreads them out, and they give her comfort and security.

5. There's a boy in her class who wears shark shirts "every day," and that freaks her out. She has a fear of sharks. Don't know what we can do about that one! ☺

Positive Comments: She likes the swings! She likes recess. She likes the art teacher but "doesn't get to have art enough," she says. She likes Gary and Sarah in her class.

I will continue on, trying to get her to school each day, but I know I won't be successful every day. I don't think Beth can attend school five days in a row. Perhaps we need to look at a shorter day schedule for her or a less than five day a week schedule. Is that even possible? I don't want her to get in the habit of not attending school, which happened last year as week after week, her special needs weren't being met (plus, it was all too overwhelming). It's hard to build a positive foundation again, but that's what we're all trying to do. Thank you for all your efforts!

The first several weeks at Heritage were rough, but Beth slowly started adjusting with our encouragement, patience, perseverance, prayer, and the school's efforts. As the weeks went on, she felt the kindness of the staff. She felt acceptance. She started trusting, and it all started to come together. She made a friend or two, and I started hearing stories about what happened at school that day.

One amazing change was that there would be no homework at

night. The school leadership realized these kids had a challenging time just getting to school each day and making it through the day. It was understood students needed plenty of time to emotionally recover at night, rest, and get ready to do it again the next day.

Do you know what I said to that? *HALLELUJAH*! What a relief for Beth and Greg and me, too. No more fighting over homework and sitting with her for hours each night.

By the second quarter of the year, she had settled in and hardly missed a day of school the rest of the year. A miracle had occurred. We had found a school home for Beth. Her public school district was worried that it wouldn't be academically challenging enough for her. It's true that the curriculum didn't meet college prep standards, but that wasn't its purpose. Beth was learning, and more importantly—she was functioning. She attended school regularly and was having academic and social success.

In ninth grade, she had to pass the Constitution test. It's a requirement to graduate. Here's what she wrote in her diary that day:

"I passed it! I passed it! The Constitution test. I passed it! I couldn't be any happier. I've been dreading it for so long. I had butterfly fairies in my stomach."

I don't know exactly what "butterfly fairies" are, but I believe her.

I can't express enough appreciation for the staff at that school, from the principal down to teachers, aides, the nurse, counselors, art and music teachers, occupational therapists, and all those I haven't mentioned. It takes a team of devoted, kind, compassionate people to manage a school, especially a school full of special-needs kids and young adults. God bless them, everyone!

The next year, Beth's school district (they were still conducting the IEP meetings) was toying with the idea of bringing Beth back to the public high school for a couple of classes. What a crazy idea! She was thriving in this private school and was there for good reason. Why would they want to disrupt it all? It almost made me ill to think about the repercussions of such a decision.

I was honest with Beth and told her what they were thinking. I didn't tell her my opinion but asked what she thought of the idea. She wanted nothing to do with it. I suggested she write a letter expressing her thoughts. I said I'd take it to the IEP meeting. Here's what my awesome teenage writer put together:

> My mom said you wanted to send me to McLean High School for some classes. I would instantly go against that because my past at the middle school was awful. I am doing fine at this school but that's because the teachers are more understanding. I am able to raise my level freely if the work isn't hard enough. I have raised my level myself and I'm proud of myself for that.
>
> I know I would not make it at McLean. The middle school was small compared to McLean. If I couldn't handle that, how do you expect me to handle McLean?
>
> I know you want me to experience the real world more, based on what my mom told me, but technically, I have a job already out in the world. I see people there and sometimes talk to them. I have a part-time job at the Bellwood library. My school got it for me. There are a lot of customers who ask me questions, and I have to tell them who to go to for help.
>
> This school isn't protected, there are still a lot of things that happen at Heritage that stress me out and yet I learned to work through them. I've learned a lot coming to this school.
>
> I actually have friends here. This school gives me what I need. The teachers are there for me. I have a great connection with the teachers. I'm very close to the teachers, actually.
>
> These are some reasons why I would not be interested in going to McLean High School. The exact same thing would happen there as happened at the middle school. Everything is so complicated.

She was right. The school district eventually agreed she was doing well in the private placement. We all heaved a sigh of relief when that meeting was over.

Middle school means drama. High school means more drama. There was a lot of drama in her school. Her diaries from those days (which I have permission to read, by the way) are full of drama.

Speaking of drama, I'll never forget the day a boy called and asked to speak to Beth. My daughter. My baby girl. *Oh no. Here we go.*

Beth talked to that boy about two hours that night, and before long, they were a couple, and she was in LUV. To be fair, I have to be grateful for this boy. She could have ended up with someone far worse. Erik was kind and patient. He put up with Beth's moods. Not many would be willing to do that. He actually was great at calming her down when she was angry or depressed. I so appreciated that help. Erik was 18 years old. *Gulp.* When they first started "dating," Beth was only 15. That concerned me. I started praying harder!

Their relationship grew, and they started hanging out at each other's homes on Saturday (with parents driving). With Beth's immaturity and impulsivity (and an 18-year-old boy with similar characteristics), I knew I needed to get Beth on birth control. As someone who loved Jesus, it was my conviction that sex was saved for marriage—one woman, one man, forever. However, Beth messed with a lot of my deeply held convictions. As impulsive as she was, I knew that she and a boy together, with plenty of time on their hands, spelled trouble. Even if I did watch them like a hawk, and I did, I knew there was no other answer. There was no way that I was risking a pregnancy because it wouldn't be Beth's baby to raise. It would be mine, and I absolutely was not up for that. Abortion wasn't an option. Adoption would send Beth over the emotional edge. So off we went to the gynecologist and got some little pills. I made sure she took her pill every day. We definitely did talk about sex and waiting for marriage. She agreed with me, in theory. But I didn't trust her—or him. Getting her on birth control was a good idea.

That was just one of the rules that got bent in my "Beth world." There were many others. Erik decided to break up with Beth at the end of the school year. This was devastating for her, resulting in her second hospitalization at the same behavioral hospital she had been in previously. Here's an email I sent to an Asperger's support group for parents about that difficult time:

As many of you have kept up with our romance saga, you know that my 16-year-old aspie is trying to work her way through a breakup, and she's having a very difficult time of it. It's been 2 months, and she is consumed by it. She's depressed and angry much of the time and can't seem to get past it. We've had several incidents this summer, such as refusing to get IN the car when we're leaving somewhere, and trying to jump OUT of the car while I was driving. We just got back from a Michigan vacation, and while much of it was good, there were incidents where she would fly off the handle, stomp out of the room or a restaurant, over NOTHING. She is on edge. Several times during vacation she demanded that we take her to the hospital as soon as we got home. She says she "needs help." She "needs help coping with tragedy." I actually respect her for realizing it and wanting to get help. Plus, we are exhausted from trying to keep up with her moods and behaviors. So, she willingly walked into the hospital yesterday, the same one she was in two years ago. We talked about options. She agreed to do the day program where she could receive therapy and counseling but come home at night. Then she decided she didn't want to start "today," but "tomorrow." She was getting cold feet. Since we were already there, and the mountains of insurance paperwork was already being processed, we knew we couldn't do that. And we didn't know if we could get her back the next day. She did need help. Well, that turned, as you might imagine, into anger, defiance, fleeing into the ladies' room, then screaming obscenities at me and others, plus a kick or two to my legs for good measure. She tried to escape, but they had already locked the front door by then (this was probably not anything new for them). She dissolved into tears but was still defiant. This was her "fight or flight" behavior. I knew she was scared to death, but she wouldn't let me near her. Yet she wanted to be by me. Sigh. We told them she was very strong and they'd need reinforcement since they were going to move her up to the girls' floor. They brought seven men to help convince her. Talk about intimidating. Then they asked Greg and me to take the elevator up to the third floor and promised they would not hurt her. As we left, I heard them consoling her, talking quietly to deescalate, coaxing her into walking up the stairs, which she eventually did.

The admission was changed from day patient to inpatient. I'm glad they saw all of that. It is the story of our lives. Guess what else? The psychiatrist put down Bipolar/Asperger's on the form for admission. So, it looks like it's becoming official, as I knew all along. I don't have to say "possibly bipolar" anymore. Her moods are all over the place. The doctors don't like to diagnose bipolar syndrome until later teens or adulthood, but I had read enough about it to predict she would get that diagnosis at some point.

It's so hard because she is so sad there. They are fairly lenient—they let her call me if she needs to—and she did, 5 times yesterday. She was very sad and crying. I took a couple of personal items over, and she requested to see me. They let us visit for 15 minutes, and she ran to me and sobbed. My heart broke, and still does, as I'm typing this. It's so hard, yet I know she needs help with her moods to get through life, and we need her to get help, so we can live with her.

The girls there are not like her. Beth is very naïve. They are experienced, hard-core street kids. I'm hoping and praying she'll find a friend more like her that will help make her stay more tolerable. Having a friend makes a huge difference for Beth.

We're waiting to hear about a staffing meeting, maybe today, where we'll discuss objectives, length of stay, etc. School starts next Wednesday, and she's very worried about getting out before then. Don't know if it will happen.

Thanks for reading if you made it through this far. I think I better now check out some "Parents of Bipolar Adolescents" online support groups. I need all the support I can get.

Beth did get released in time for school, but the drama continued between her and Erik throughout the year. They were off and on, and eventually, Erik graduated a year ahead of Beth, so they didn't see each other as much. Probably a good thing.

A career coach at the school went into the community and found jobs for the capable seniors to help them get a taste of working in the real world. The goal was to equip the students to hold down a job, contribute to society, and provide income. He found a job for Beth at a local library. (She mentioned it earlier in her letter to McLean High School.) She assisted in the office with stamping books and other jobs, working one or two afternoons a week. It was a great experience for her. The library even allowed her to work in the summer, so they must have valued her contributions.

One day, Beth told me she was tired of working at the library, and she wanted to work at Target.

I had learned that I shouldn't jump when Beth talked about wanting to do something. She talked about a lot of things. If she repeated it again and again, then I started paying attention.

She did tell me, again and again, she wanted to work at Target. We lived about three miles from a Target, so that would be convenient because I'd have to take her and pick her up, and it was much closer than the library. I just couldn't see her handling a job there, but I hated to squelch her enthusiasm. Greg and I always encouraged her to try whatever she set her heart on doing. Because of that, I helped her fill out the online application. Actually, I filled out the application on the computer in the store. Even the application was difficult for her to understand.

When we left, I thought we were done. We had filled it out, and now there was nothing else we could do. *Hopefully, she'll just let it go and forget about Target.*

Wrong! They called her and set up an interview time. I had filled out the application thoroughly, and they thought she had done it. She had been employed at a library, showing she was employable. Now what were we going to do?

I believe if a door opens, you walk through it. So, I took a deep breath, drove her to the interview, and waited in the waiting area. I knew she was nervous about it, and I felt very anxious for her. This was her first "real" interview, not prearranged through her school. I prayed for her, for calmness. I knew she wouldn't give appropriate responses but figured the interview experience would be good for her.

She would just have to learn the hard way that we don't always get what we want in life, I thought to myself.

The young, cute male HR guy came out after a while, with Beth behind him. She had papers in her hand. She would be starting the next week as a cashier.

A cashier?! What just happened? My jaw was hanging open as she smiled at me and told me the news.

I could not believe she had interviewed effectively and was offered a job on the spot—a cashier job!

This is the girl who has trouble looking at people in the eye, talking with them, and counting money? Are you kidding me? I was incredulous. Counting money was one of her weakest skills. I bet they didn't test that in the interview!

But just as she had wanted, she started working at Target as a cashier. Fortunately, she told me that most people paid for their purchases with a credit or debit card. They taught her what she needed to know, and she did the job satisfactorily. Sometimes when I came to pick her up, I'd sneak in and hide behind the displays and just watch her in action, thinking, *This is Beth. This is our daughter. She's interacting with people. She's a cashier. Unbelievable.*

I'm sure some monetary errors were made during those months, but I never heard about them. A few months later, Beth grew tired of the cashier job and wanted to do something different at Target. This is a common theme for mentally ill people. I told her to ask the HR man who hired her if there were other options, like stocking shelves. She said she asked, but nothing ever changed. So, she decided she was done. Nothing I could say could change her mind.

We had been talking about signing her up for a private driver's education class, so she used that as an excuse and told the manager she couldn't fit working at Target in her schedule because she had to take a driver's ed class. That was the end of Target.

Beth landing that job at Target was one of the biggest shocks of my life. There have been many Beth shocks, both positive and negative, so that's saying a lot. As I thought about the Target episode, I think it may have been God telling me, "You don't know it all, Maralee Parker. You think you have this all figured out, but that's not the case. You wait and see."

People have asked me why Beth can't work. She "looks" somewhat normal. She's had a couple of short-lived jobs. The problem is, she can't keep it going. It takes a lot of energy for her to get up early, make herself presentable, get to the job, try to understand what is expected of her, try to "act normal" around all of the people, do a good enough job to not get fired, go home, and do it all over again the next day. Even a part-time job would be difficult. It creates a tremendous amount of stress and anxiety to be employed, and while she may be able to do it for a short time, she can't maintain it.

She often doesn't understand what is expected of her but is unable to ask a question to clarify expectations. In all of her years of schooling, she never once raised her hand to ask a question or answer a question, to my knowledge (I've asked teachers). Her anxiety controls her. It doesn't make sense to us who don't struggle with it. But I've seen this displayed throughout her life. So, if she doesn't understand what is expected, she gets confused and overwhelmed, leading to even more anxiety and then … giving up.

After her Target experience, Beth had a birthday and was 18 years old, but we weren't entirely confident she was ready for driver's education. We didn't know if she would be capable of driving. She was physically able, but we questioned whether she could mentally make quick judgment calls when needed. What would she do if she had a flat tire? Had an accident? Had someone yell at her out of road rage? But Greg and I believed we shouldn't go through life thinking of worst-case scenarios and holding her back if she truly could drive. We wanted to support her in life—as far as she could go.

She decided she wanted to learn to drive, so we proceeded. Even though it was less expensive, we knew it would add to her anxiety to try to fit her into the overpopulated public-school schedule for their driver's ed program, so we elected to go to a small, private driving school.

I helped her study the rules of the road. I felt she was ready to take the printed test at the DMV. We went and she passed. She had completed the first step. (Yikes!)

It was time for behind-the-wheel education. On the first night, I drove her to the class, walked in with her, introduced her to the instructor, and left. All of this was very hard for Beth (and me), but she wanted to drive, and she forced herself to do what she needed to do to achieve that goal.

God sent an angel to Beth that night. Her name was Alyssa. Beth and Alyssa just happened to sit at the same two-person table. During the class, Beth noticed Alyssa was sketching anime characters. Anime (Japanese animated shows) had become one of Beth's new obsessions in her teen years, and she was very intrigued and pleased to see the sketches.

At break time, Alyssa started talking to her. Beth would never start a conversation, but she would respond if someone else started it. They talked about anime, and the rest is history! Beth looked forward to class. Alyssa offered to buy a DQ blizzard for Beth at break time the next week. That gave Beth confidence, thinking maybe, just maybe, Alyssa liked her. Beth was excited to have a new friend who even loved anime. She had her behind-the-wheel driving hours with Alyssa, too, which pleased her immensely. She successfully finished the course. (Yikes!) Now she just needed to get her license at the DMV.

What follows is another one of those unbelievable Beth moments, forever imprinted in my mind. I took her to a smaller nearby town, a smaller DMV, which I thought might make her less anxious. I guided her through all the necessary hoops once we arrived. The examiner called her name, and I watched her walk off, and I prayed, *Please, Lord, don't let her crash my car!* Well, maybe I wasn't that explicit, but I definitely was praying for her.

She passed. Unbelievable. My daughter now had a driver's license. (Imagine Macaulay Culkin's *Home Alone* shaving face here.)

That was a good thing and a scary thing. She could drive herself to where she needed to go. I didn't have to chauffeur her. This was good. But she could go wherever she wanted now with more independence. That might not be so good. I'm sure all parents have those feelings when their teen gets their license. We worried more with Beth because of her immaturity and anger issues.

One terrifying experience happened a few months after she got her license. One day she was daydreaming, and after leaving her school, she accidentally took the entrance ramp toward Chicago instead of the next one—the usual one that led to our home. She eventually realized she wasn't recognizing landmarks and had no idea where she was, as cars were whizzing by. She struggles big time with directions. (This was before the days of GPS on phones.) She drove based on landmarks, not road names.

Our phone rang. "I think I took a wrong turn, and I'm on a busy road, but I don't know where I am! And my phone is almost dead!" She's screaming by this time as the panic grew.

Anytime my phone rang with Beth's ringtone song "We Are Family," my heart beat faster. I never knew what I'd hear from her. This was a perfect example.

Here she was, after dark, 9 p.m., driving on a very busy road, *somewhere*. I took a deep breath, tried to remain calm, and tried to calm her. This was challenging because one of my phobias was driving on the interstate with all of those big green and white signs. But this wasn't about me; this was about Beth.

I started asking what traffic signs she was passing to better understand what road she was on. She said she passed something that said "O'Hare" and "Northwest Suburbs." I put her on speakerphone and told her to keep reading the signs to me. Greg was listening now too. He knows much more about the Chicagoland traffic maze than I, who am also directionally challenged. Eventually, he caught something that helped him know about where she was, so he told her to pull off the side of the road, lock her doors, and put her hazard lights on.

We took off in Greg's truck, and we prayed. When we got near the area Greg thought she might be, we started looking for her little tan car. We eventually found her—and her dead phone. *Thank You, God!*

This girl ages us. Every gray hair is legitimately earned.

Beth persevered through the rest of high school and was even able to finish in February of her senior year, having accumulated enough credits to graduate. She walked the aisle in June with the rest of her class.

Beth wrote this journal entry at the end of her high school years:

> Life got hard at times but I always made it. My boyfriend helped me and supported me and comforted me when I needed it. He is a great friend and boyfriend to me and I love him as I love everyone who has helped me in this school. My life was really horrible before I got to this school. I have grown so much people say, and have matured a lot over the few years I was here.
>
> Now my view on life is that we all have a reason we are here. God will help us through any hard times and he will show us the way. We all have friends that will be there for us and a family who will always love us. My mom and dad have put up with a lot with me and continue to help me and love me. I love them a lot. My brother and sister-in-law have also helped me through a lot and I love them to. You will always find love in your life through the people close to you.
>
> You should never even think to give up your life. No matter how hard things will get. Don't give up your faith in God. He will always believe in you, as will your family and friends. Trust is crucial in life. You can't trust everyone but don't be afraid to trust the ones you know who truly love you. The teachers in this school have

helped me through a lot and so have my friends. I couldn't have done it without any of them.

Remember God is in control and He will help you.

She was in a good emotional place when she graduated. She had changed so much from the girl we had to drag to this new school five years earlier.

High school was over! We celebrated this huge milestone in her life. Now the best was yet to come, right? The world was her oyster. Isn't that the way it works? ♥

12

Oh, the Places You'll Go

With apologies to Dr. Seuss, this chapter's title fits my life with Beth when she was a teen and young adult. As difficult as her early years were with the sleep issues, defiance, meltdowns, and school challenges, the post-graduation time was even more challenging. The issues were bigger.

Normally, our kids graduate from high school, then go on to college or find a job, and settle into a new chapter in their lives. Some may marry shortly after high school. These next steps often don't fall into place for people like Beth. It's hard for them to watch their friends move on (if they have friends) because they know it may not happen for them. Anxiety and depression are common during this transition time.

It took a while for Beth to acclimate to not having the school structure. She'd been in that routine for the vast majority of her life. It became clear that fall after high school graduation that her life would be very different now. She missed her friends and the teachers. Her school friends lived far from the school and were bussed in, so it was difficult to get together. She remained friends with one girl, Jenna, who lived within 10 miles of us. Their friendship deepened. At first, I was glad she had a friend. Everyone needs a friend.

I'll never forget the day I received a call while at work. Beth was at the police station. She had been arrested for shoplifting! She and Jenna had been at the mall and together decided to steal two pairs of jeans from a women's store. They had a shopping bag and slid the jeans into that bag while they were in the try-on room. When they stepped out into the mall, store personnel detained them until security arrived. Beth told me that Jenna had told her what to do, but Beth was "left holding the bag," so she was the one charged. I believed her because Jenna had been bragging to Beth about other things she had stolen.

I burst into tears when she told me where she was, and what had happened. I was an hour away, so I had time to contemplate as I drove to get her. My heart was broken, but I determined I would be kind and not judgmental when I saw her. The bigger discussion could wait until we got home. I was talking to God as I drove. *Oh, Lord! What else? What else are we going to go through with this girl? I don't know how much more I can handle.*

It was a dangerous question.

We were newbies in the court system. We decided we would hire a lawyer to help us navigate. He was helpful and expensive. We tried to prepare for the court date. But how do you prepare an autistic, developmentally-delayed, immature girl with huge anxiety issues? She was scared to death. I was, too.

The Second Chance Program option was offered to Beth. This was the best scenario. She would need to attend four two-hour class sessions at the county judicial center. I didn't know if she could do it or would do it. She became confused and overwhelmed quickly and then would shut down. I was hoping for the best and praying she would get through it.

Since this was her first offense, and the court was told mental illness and intellectual challenge were involved, they only required the classes without community service. So "we" did the class with me waiting in the back of the room (if I hadn't, she wouldn't have attended) every Thursday night for four weeks. It was a room of mostly teenagers, probably arrested for the same type of offense, I'm guessing.

Once that was finished, I gently encouraged Beth to apply for a job. We talked about different possibilities. She needed a job she could do and enjoy, but I wasn't sure if she could be successful at any job. After discussing it, she decided she might like working in a daycare center and let me help her apply to several. She knew this was the next step for her life, but she wasn't sure she could handle it. Anxiety was ever-present. Every day. I reminded her it was another opportunity to just take life "one day at a time." Throughout her life, I'd been teaching her that approach as she dealt with her anxieties.

You may wonder why I applied for her, instead of insisting, like a good parent, that she do the application work herself. I did it because I didn't believe it would happen if I didn't. I don't think she would have filled out the applications. If Beth did, the employer would see her child-like printing, which probably would have provided a negative first impression. Because of her proprioception issues, her handwriting always resembles that of a young child.

I filled out the applications because I was trying to help her get her foot in the door, to help her have an opportunity to move forward in life. She needed a job not only for the money but also for the encouragement it would provide for her to get out of bed each day. It would boost her self-esteem and give her purpose. Maybe she would be able to make a new friend or two.

We were thrilled when a daycare center called her for an interview. I went with her (she wouldn't go otherwise) and waited in the car.

She got the job! Again, I was shocked and very happy, but inwardly I worried. *Here we go again.*

I had no idea if she would be able to do what was required or if she would even understand what was required. But if she didn't try, we'd never know. She was appropriate enough in the interview to get hired, so I was hoping that was a good sign of future success.

She started the job and actually enjoyed it. Structure is always good for her, and this provided much-needed structure. She had to go to bed at a decent hour to get up early and be ready for work. She needed to have her outfit ready. She was proud of herself for getting a job. Things were going well.

Until they weren't.

Her supervisor spoke to her at work one day, explaining that her fingerprints from her background check showed that she had been arrested (the shoplifting arrest), and until that was removed from her record, she could no longer work there. Beth was confused. We went back together to pick up some paperwork, and the owner explained again (to both of us). She was apologetic, but she needed to follow the legal procedures of the organization. She was just a franchise owner. She encouraged Beth to return once she got the arrest expunged from her record.

This made Beth feel a little better. She had an invitation to come back, so she thought she must have been doing a good job.

"Do you see how that arrest is causing a problem now?" I lamented. In her immaturity, I didn't think Beth realized how seriously her "record" would affect her life. She had continued having urges to steal, she told me. I prayed she would quickly realize what a bad idea that would be. *Lord, please give her the understanding and strength to resist those urges!*

We worked on getting the arrest expunged. She had finished the Second Chance Program. That was the first step. We then had to wait a length of time, then contact the lawyer again to get the legal process underway. I should say, "proce$$."

Eventually, we were successful. Beth was able to apply for another daycare job (the first center she worked at had closed), and again, I was shocked when she got a call for an interview. She was hired and worked for this daycare center for five months. I was so proud of her and amazed that she was doing it, day after day. She was totally thrown for a loop when something out of the ordinary was expected, like attending a group meeting off campus. She couldn't drive anywhere but directly to the daycare center—the same way every time. Fortunately, with my help, she was able to get a ride to the special meeting with a coworker, but even that caused great anxiety. (I imagine the coworker thinking, *What 20 year old needs her mother to help get her a ride?*)

A few months after she started working, the very kind and approachable director who hired Beth moved on, and a new boss arrived. She was very different from the first director.

Shortly after that, Beth came home one Friday, confused. She said she had been called to a meeting with the director. A parent had complained that she saw Beth grab a two-year-old's wrist, and it "left a mark." Beth does have issues with her muscle strength. She doesn't realize how hard she is pressing. It's that proprioception thing again.

"What did the director say?" I asked as she tried to remember. Beth wasn't sure what she had heard or what it meant. She was overwhelmed, and that usually led to a complete shutdown. I called the director, with Beth nearby. After I explained Beth's confusion, the director would not talk to me because of HIPAA privacy issues. I had sensed Beth's job was in jeopardy, so I took the direct approach and asked, "Should she come to work on Monday morning?"

She told me there would need to be an investigation and procedures to follow. I knew Beth couldn't handle that, nor would she want to go back there after all of the stress and anxiety of an investigation, even if she was cleared of the charge. She doesn't do well with criticism.

Beth decided she was done. "If she wants to resign, without an investigation, she'll need to send a resignation letter." I helped her compose it. That was the end of that job.

Beth then decided she'd take a break from the working world. But soon, she was getting bored of sleeping around the clock and watching TV. "Mom, what do you think about me going to college at MCC?" I knew that was probably not going to work. She wouldn't be able to handle the work, the lectures, and the noisy environment. But it was all "talk" at this point. It's good to dream. I didn't want to burst her bubble.

"Well, maybe you could try taking just one class in child development. You seem to like the daycare setting and learning about kids. You could try it and see if it worked out."

A class might be helpful and look good on her resume if she were to get another job in daycare. Just as important, she needed something to fill her time, give her purpose, and help her get out of bed in the morning.

"Mom, could you go with me?"

"I can't go with you and stay in the room, but I could go the first time or two and wait somewhere nearby," I told her. Going to class would be challenging for her on several levels, but I was very supportive of her, seeing if she could succeed.

She decided to try one class. I tried to pave the way to help her be successful. I made an appointment with the counseling department, and we both went to explain Beth's special needs. They told us of adaptations that Beth would be entitled to, such as having longer times for testing and so on. After considering it, Beth wanted to go for it. I enrolled her in an evening class. We went to the bookstore and bought the textbook. She was a college student!

On the first night of class, we walked the long walk from the parking lot to the correct building and found Classroom 4G. I was able to have a private moment with the teacher, quickly explaining Beth's special needs. She probably thought I was a helicopter parent—no doubt. I waved goodbye and walked to the lounge area, not far away. At break time, Beth came out and seemed excited but said there was a lot she didn't understand. She showed me her syllabus.

I took her back for the second class two days later. At the break, she walked up to me, head hanging down. "I have no idea what she's talking about, Mom. She uses words I've never heard of. I can't keep up. Forget it."

It wasn't surprising, but we were proud of her for trying. We had to be willing to let her fail, so we'd learn how far she could go. Nothing ventured, nothing gained.

I wrote a letter of explanation to the college, and they graciously refunded our money. The really nice thing was when she tried another class a year later, they refunded our money again—but told us it was the last time they could do that. Beth's college career had ended. At least she tried.

Shortly after Beth got her driver's license, we had invested in a Ford Escort for her. We were cautiously happy for her, hoping she could handle driving and praying God would send angels to surround her car for her benefit and those around her.

She had one accident, two spin-outs on ice, four tickets, and two warnings in four years. On a single day, she received a ticket for not stopping completely at a stop sign, one for speeding, and a warning for not having her headlights on. The last officer had her get out and attempt to walk a straight line. She experiences tremors as a side effect of her meds, so she comes off a bit shaky at times. The officer finally believed her because he only gave her a warning ticket about the headlights.

She had to go to traffic school for the tickets, and, of course, she needed me to go with her. There were about 50 people in the large room, and she was very irritated throughout the session. Her meds weren't helping her much during that period, so she was angry often, especially in a situation like this. In the car, she would scream, "I'm NOT going! They can go f— themselves. I'm done. DONE!" She took her fear, stress, and frustration out on me, of course. I tried to calmly encourage her. At the last minute, she did get out of the car and walk in, but she was far from emotionally stable. At the break, she was ready to walk out again.

I begged her to stick it out so she could keep her license. "This isn't optional, Beth. It's required. You're over halfway done. Just hang in there." I didn't know if she was going to go back or not. I had learned many times that I couldn't control this girl. She finally did trudge back to the room. If you could have seen her face—it was not pretty. She was furious. It wasn't just her frustration at having to "earn" her license back, but anxiety, which always displayed as anger. She was experiencing much fear and frustration that day. She had sensory overstimulation by the sheer number of people there, the unknown classroom setting and physical closeness of the chairs, and the curriculum that was incomprehensible to her. It all contributed to her angry mood. She did finish the class, but she was seething as we walked to the parking lot. She exploded, threw down the paperwork on the ground, yelled profanities at me, and took off running. This was in a busy, suburban shopping area. She took off running across four lanes of traffic.

This was not the first time she had run away, and it certainly wouldn't be the last. But every time, I would jump in my car and try to keep my eyes on her so I could follow her at a distance. She was 20 years old by now but had the maturity level of a 12-year-old. Her mental illness seemed to prevent her from thinking logically. It was so frustrating for Greg and me as we tried to reason with her.

This time was more challenging. The setting was much more dangerous because of the busy traffic. She had no idea where she was.

Oh, Lord, I need help again! I had no clue how this was going to end. I just had to stay in the moment, try to stay calm, pray, and keep my eyes on her as I drove, trying to not frustrate other drivers behind me or get in an accident. When she would see my car, she'd take off in another direction. Do you realize how difficult it is to turn around on a busy four-way divided highway on a Saturday? I did lose her at times but kept searching, and eventually, I'd see her again. *Thank you, God!*

I saw her duck into a clothing store in a strip mall. I was able to get parked and get in the store before she left. I wasn't sure what would happen. This is when my years of "lived" psychological expertise came in handy. I knew I needed to deescalate the situation. When I found her, she was calmly looking at some shirts. I started casually looking at some clothes nearby, but not at the same rack. After a few seconds, I said, "Oh, look at this one. Isn't it cute?"

"It's okay, but I like this one better," she replied in a flat tone.

"Oh yeah, that one is cute, too," I agreed. *Help, Lord.*

It was over. As quickly as it had come, the meltdown was over. We looked around a little more, walked to the car, and drove home. I didn't even have to buy anything to seal the deal.

I thanked God. He had answered my prayers—again.

These meltdowns were incredibly stressful for both of us, but Beth usually moved on from them rather quickly. On the other hand, I had heart palpitations when I was searching for her and hidden jubilation when she responded to me about the "cute shirt" because I knew we had turned a corner. By the time we arrived home, I was spent. It was emotionally exhausting on a regular basis with my girl.

If you have a child like this, I want you to know you're not alone. It's a crazy way to live. It's exhausting and very frustrating. It's more challenging if you have other children in your home. It requires a ridiculous amount of patience, perseverance, forgiveness, and love. Keep reminding yourself that your child's brain is broken. Much of their behavior results from that broken brain. It's incredibly challenging for us, as parents, to navigate, but can you imagine what it's like for them? Take a few minutes and think about what it might be like to live inside your kid's head 24/7. That might create more empathy for them. (This is best done when you're not in a crisis situation or recovering from one.)

After Beth lost the second daycare job, she retreated into our home for quite a while. She loved Japanese anime and poured herself into this as her autistic obsession. She read books, watched anime on TV, and read "fanfics" (stories about anime) on the computer. She even wrote some fanfics. She printed out pictures of her anime characters in full color. Between the fanfics and pictures, she would print stacks of paper. My frugal, logical mind had trouble investing so much money on expensive printer ink, but as I mentioned before, I told myself that she had nothing else going on in life. She didn't buy clothes, jewelry, makeup, or birthday gifts for friends. She didn't take dance lessons or buy illegal drugs. So, we spent money on printer ink. It occupied her and gave her joy.

She went to her first anime convention with Alyssa, that friend from her driver's education class. That anime con experience opened the door for many more to come. Thousands of kids dress up in cosplay (costumes) of their favorite anime characters. It's quite a sight to behold! Soon Alyssa started working and could not attend the cons, so guess who occasionally went with Beth? Thus, the title of this chapter, "Oh, the Places You'll Go!" At least a half a dozen times, I found myself at a hotel, amid hundreds of costumed teens and young adults, symbolically patting myself on the back as "mother of the year." I attended voice-actor panels with Beth and accompanied her to the vendor shopping area, where you could find anime characters on visors, keychains, and T-shirts. It was definitely a place I'd never find myself if Beth wasn't my daughter.

We even flew to Texas for an anime convention. She wanted to attend it because her favorite voice actor, Vic Mignonia, would be there. The reason I agreed was to tie in a visit to some good friends who had moved to that area. I also wanted to give her something to anticipate. She has always needed a symbolic carrot dangling in front of her to keep her happy. The thought of an airplane trip and seeing Vic at an anime convention kept her going for months.

The trip turned out well. We had fun in the hotel, just Mom and daughter. One memorable moment was when we used an eyelash curler to get the top off of a sparkling grape juice bottle. We had no tools, so we had to improvise. We were successful! It was a funny moment we'll always remember, and we have pictures.

Beth enjoyed the convention, although all she really cared about was attending Vic's panels and getting yet another autograph and hug from him. That convention was extra special because she and I volunteered and were chosen by Vic to help him sell his CDs in his autograph line. We sat at a table right behind him, so after he greeted his fans, they walked by our table. We were "insiders!" It was an awesome experience for Beth.

When it came time to return home, our friends drove us to the airport. We had conveniently dropped off our luggage at the curb and were heading to the security line.

"Beth, you'll need your driver's license for the security check."

"I put it in my wallet. It's in my suitcase. I didn't think I'd need it."

I'm not a screamer, but if I were, I would have screamed at that moment. Instead, this was yet another opportunity not to panic and just address the situation logically and calmly. Airport security was very tight at that time, so I had to explain why my "adult" daughter did not have her ID. Then they escorted her somewhere (without me) and asked her questions, such as, "What is the closest intersection to your home address?" That would be like asking Beth, "What essential purpose does a catalytic converter accomplish?"

She would never be able to answer geographical questions like that. She "turns at McDonald's, and then goes to Dunkin, and then passes Target to get to Walmart." She gets around via landmarks. I knew she was freaking out as they questioned her. I had alerted them to her disabilities. It was another great opportunity to pray, which I did. I think they finally gave up, realizing she wasn't a threat. She had to be patted down, and eventually, they let her through. *Thank you, Lord!* I chalked it up to another unbelievable "Beth story."

Beth also loves horror movies. I don't. She especially loves weird, Japanese horror movies like *The Ring*. I love my daughter, and years ago, I did go with her to several of those yucky movies. All in the name of love. Oh, the places you'll go!

Beth decided she wanted a tattoo. I made her wait until she was 18, but I couldn't prohibit it after that. Tattoos had become very chic. A couple of her friends had them. I tried to rationally (what was I thinking?) explain that tattoos are with you forever, even if you don't like them anymore. Nonetheless, the day came when she got her first tattoo around her ankle, and I went with her. I'm really not a tattoo parlor type of gal, but I love my daughter. During this period, she continued to be in a dark place, entertained suicidal thoughts, and was cutting her arms to release emotional pain. I was willing to do uncomfortable things to provide some diversion for her, even if it involved tattoo parlors.

She loved her first tattoo and went on to get several more, including having the words "Justin Bieber" added near a butterfly tattoo on her back. She loved Justin Bieber.

"He helped me through a hard time in my life." She and her friend did that without telling me. That was the challenge with her having independence with her own car.

"Oh, Beth. Now that's going to be with you the rest of your life."

"I know, Mom. I know."

Remember the phrase I said to Beth as she worried and stressed about things? "One day at a time." There were plenty of opportunities to remind her and me to focus on the present and not worry about the future. Matthew 6:34 in the Bible says it so well: "So don't worry about tomorrow, for tomorrow will bring its own worries. Today's trouble is enough for today."

Beth heard "One day at a time" from me often. So, on one adventurous day a few years ago, it only made sense that we both marched off to a tattoo parlor and had "One day at a time" matching tattoos inked into our skin. At 63, that was my first of two tattoos, and it was a very meaningful one. I have no regrets. In fact, that tattoo has become a wonderful teaching visual as I'm encouraging others, and it's always so convenient right there on my arm! Oh, the places you'll go.

For curious minds, my second tat was an infinity symbol with paw prints. (I knew some of you were wondering.)

There were other ongoing diversions in her life. We frequented the neighborhood Goodwill stores regularly. Beth loved to get something new, and shopping at the mall became too expensive. Goodwill clothes made her happy. She could afford to get a couple of things there. We visited Goodwill stores in several nearby towns and still do. I wouldn't normally be a Goodwill shopper, but I am now.

She also got into a mermaid phase. Somehow, she learned about vinyl mermaid fins you put over your feet so that you can swim like a mermaid. Over the years, she has purchased at least five of these (they crack or wear out), and she also paid our seamstress friend to make mermaid "tails" for her that she'd pull over her fin and up to her waist. She actually resembled a mermaid! I was somewhat fearful at first because she's not the best swimmer, but she hasn't drowned yet, and she's been playing around with her mermaid fins for years now. It was another obsession for her. She just bought a new one, so the obsession hasn't left yet.

I've explained how pets have played such a big role in Beth's life and still do. She currently has a dog, a bunny, and two rats. Let me tell you the hamster cremation story. This is definitely a place where I had no intention of going.

She had a beloved hamster who died. She was devastated. She talked out her grief with me and said she wanted to get it cremated. I kindly responded (while inwardly rolling my eyes) that it was too expensive to cremate. Who cremates hamsters? She tried to persuade me, but I was resolute—in a kind way.

That evening, while we were sleeping, she proceeded to get a shoebox and try to cremate her dead hamster herself on our back patio.

It didn't work so well.

She was even more upset after that. She had a dead, half-burned hamster in a box. To calm her down, I agreed I would call to see how much it would cost for professional cremation. After several calls, I found a place that worked with veterinarians who would do it for $75. It hurt to pay $75, but this had become a huge emotional issue for her. I did make her pay for some of it.

The plan went like this: I was told to meet this guy in a red Explorer in the outskirts of the nearby Walmart parking lot the following Thursday at 9:30 a.m. When the day came, I located him and gave him the box and the money. I felt like a drug dealer exchanging "the goods."

The following Thursday, as he was on his way to pick up cremation orders from the same vet, he explained he would again meet me in said Walmart to give me the finished product. It happened as planned. Again, I felt like a drug dealer. But Beth got her little cremated hamster in a box, and she seemed to be appreciative and at peace.

Another chapter in our lives involved horses. We have a family friend who first introduced Beth to horses when Beth was in middle school. Beth so enjoyed going to the barn with Amy. She never lost her fondness for horses, so in her late teens, when she needed something to do, I signed her up for equine therapy. I knew that would make her happy. She spent time with a wonderful woman and a safe horse on a regular basis, learning the basics of horsemanship.

After a while, Beth wanted to "shareboard" a horse. For those outside of the horse world, that means you find someone who wants to share their horse with you, and you pay for part of the boarding expense, which is not inexpensive. I researched it and thought maybe it could work if we found just the right horse owner (who would have compassion with Beth) and horse. Beth went online to research. She found a lady who was advertising for a shareboarder. It was an amazing opportunity because this owner wasn't doing it for the money. She wanted someone to spend time with her horse because she couldn't. She was recovering from cancer. She charged a pittance, and Beth started shareboarding her sweet horse, named Maiya. *Thank you, God.*

After a year of shareboarding, Maiya's owner had to stop the agreement because she had relatives who wanted to shareboard. Beth had trouble finding another similar situation that was nearby and affordable. Then she got the wild idea of buying her own horse. She researched pasture board and indoor board at a dozen or more area barns. She became obsessed, which she is so prone to do. She couldn't think of anything else, and she had nothing in her life to distract her. She campaigned loud and strong.

So much so that I started kicking the possibility around in my head. *Could we? Should we? Would this be a wonderful hobby to fill Beth's empty life? Or an extravagant expense we'd be "saddled" with? Would she get thrown off and die?*

I thought of it all.

Beth was 23 by this time, but again, very immature. Life had been so difficult for her since high school graduation. I wanted to encourage her to find an interest in anything to help her from falling deeper into depression.

Beth even created a contract, promising to sacrifice for the needs of her horse, not yell so much, help out more around the house, and so on. Then she signed her name—in cursive! But could she possibly fulfill those promises? Not a chance.

Greg and I discussed it, thought about it, and prayed about it. This was a huge decision! In the end, Greg pretty much left it up to me. We both realized I would be the one supervising it all, transporting Beth several times a week and managing the horse's care.

Greg and I also added her car into the mix. After much discussion, we agreed that although Beth passed her driving test successfully and we wanted independence for her, she was not a safe driver. We didn't want her to get hurt, and we didn't want her to hurt anyone. She was so impulsive, which is not good when you're behind a steering wheel. She was also prone to jump in her car and take off (fast) when she was angry. We decided we'd ask her to give up her car and driving, though giving up driving would hugely impact her life in the future. We said if she was willing to do that, we would sell the car and put that money toward a horse purchase. We tied the two things together, the positive of getting a horse, and the negative of giving up driving. We weren't sure we were doing the right thing. Do parents ever know for sure?

We presented the proposal to her, and it didn't take her long to agree to it. We started researching online more seriously, checking out horses within our budget. I wanted it to be a small horse so she wouldn't have as far to fall!

The "horse chapter" of our lives truly took me places I never dreamed of. I grew up on a farm until I was 10 years old. I love animals. We had cows, pigs, chickens, cats, and a dog, but no horses. Years before, my dad had used horses in the fields. I have a picture of him, my mom, and the horses by a plow. But that was long before I was born. I had no clue about horses.

We found a possibility, a large pony, and went to see her. Beth fell in love immediately. She was flashy, a black and white paint, and affordable. (Owning a horse doesn't break the bank on the day of purchase. It's the monthly board afterward that accomplishes that.) We hired Rachel, the equine therapy expert Beth had worked with earlier, to come and take a look at the pony. We needed the advice of someone who knew horses. Rachel felt she was "sound," which meant she didn't see any obvious defects in her. We also had a vet come out and do a pre-purchase exam. She tested out okay. My only concern was the size of the pony. Was Beth too big for her? The vet felt it would be okay since Beth was just going to pleasure ride and not jump or use her in competition.

So—just like that—we became horse owners. We named her "Lacey," short for "Laces of Hope." It was a fitting name. She did give Beth hope.

We quickly learned some horse lingo. We learned about farriers, Coggins tests, and teeth floating. We learned about shots, chaps, girths, halters, and bits. We learned about stirrups and saddles, hackamores, fly masks and colic. We learned about gaits: walking, trotting, cantering (but not galloping!). We learned about tack and cooling blankets and warming blankets. We learned about treats—lots and lots of treats.

Beth was such a proud horse owner. We had learned a lot, but we were still very, very green. We tried our best but were very appreciative of other more seasoned horse owners who helped us along the way.

We owned Lacey for about a year, but Beth started having problems with Lacey's behavior. Lacey was "butt bumping" (that's what I called it) when Beth rode her, and it made Beth feel like Lacey might buck her off. I wondered again if Beth was too big for her. By this time, we had transferred Lacey to three different barns, because something had happened at each barn that made Beth uncomfortable. We asked for advice from some of the more experienced horse owners and ultimately decided to sell Lacey and get a bigger horse. It wasn't easy letting her go, but the day came when her new owner picked her up, which was the end of the Lacey era.

We found a new horse in a rural area, about an hour away. He was a beautiful paint quarter horse, also flashy, like Lacey, but he was brown and black and white. He was definitely bigger than Lacey. Beth rode him and liked him. The owners were awesome people. They had us sign a contract that stated if we ever decided to sell the horse, they would have the first right of refusal. That meant they really did love him and wanted what was best for him.

By this time, we had found another horse "expert," and we had her come out to give her opinion on this new horse. We had a vet check him out as well. He passed the test, and again, we were horse owners. Beth named him Prince.

Being a horse owner was totally unexpected, like so many other chapters in life. If someone had said I would have owned two horses when I was close to 60, I'd say, "Right. And pigs can fly, too."

As horse owners, we were at the

horse barn regularly. Very regularly. This was Beth's life now, and she was obsessed, as usual. Of course, Beth didn't drive anymore, so I took her and waited for her three to four times a week. Summer, fall, winter, and spring. Those winter days were often brutal. I didn't want to be in a smelly horse barn at 8 p.m. when it was 20 degrees out (or colder) with howling winds, figuring out how to keep the horse's water bucket from freezing. No, I didn't. I wanted to be home, snuggled in my PJs in my recliner, with a blanket over me. Nor did I want to be there when it was 90 degrees outside, but I did it because I loved my daughter. I did it because she had found a new identity as a horse owner. She talked with a few barn people here and there but didn't make any close friends. But owning a horse gave her purpose and responsibility to a living thing, which depended on her when she couldn't find any other purpose.

We moved from barn to barn over the next few months. Beth grew disgruntled with barns for one reason or another (similar to jobs) and felt there must be a better place, a more inexpensive place, a closer place, a barn with less drama. She just wanted a good fit. That was hard to find. Beth didn't always like to follow the rules, and sometimes she was scolded for doing something wrong. She felt criticism very deeply. She would replay it in her mind. It would fester and grow into something huge, and soon she didn't want to be there anymore. It was very stressful for me, as I tried to mediate between Beth's needs, the barn's requirements, and the barn owner. It was indeed a challenge.

The last placement we had for Prince was 45 minutes away, out in the country. Beth had decided to "pasture board" him. That meant he lived in the pasture, day and night. There was a shelter he could go to for protection from wind, rain, or snow, but otherwise, he was outdoors. It was significantly less expensive than boarding inside the barn. Fortunately, Prince loved it. That's what he had been used to at the previous owner's home. Unfortunately, it seemed to make him a wild boy. His behavior changed, and he didn't want to listen to Beth. He started to show attitude, and she became frustrated. Eventually, she reluctantly chose to sell him back to his original owners.

She couldn't handle the goodbye. She just wanted it to be over. She was very sad. So, yes, it was good old Mom who drove out to the barn

Maralee Parker

to meet the buyers, take care of the business deal, and say goodbye to Prince. It was sad but also a huge relief for me.

Beth and I spent two or three years pouring our lives into horses, and I don't regret it. It was a lot of work, required a great deal of commitment, and was expensive. I enjoyed being around those majestic creatures, up close and personal. I learned a lot. This horse ownership period had served its purpose for Beth. So, what was next? ♥

13
Dangerous Impulsivity

The title of this book is fitting for our journey with Beth. We never knew what was ahead. We needed to be flexible and go with the flow. Our own plans and desires came second and only if everything was calm with Beth.

We could be enjoying a (short) period of relative calm when suddenly another crisis would erupt, which was often because Beth was so impulsive. Her ADHD explained her short attention span. She didn't think before she acted or reacted. This got her (and us) into many difficult situations, some as a result of her anger, and some just because of her "stinkin' thinkin'."

One day when she was about 20, we were in the car, and she started talking about music and iTunes in particular. Beth loved music. It was therapeutic for her. But she did not have a credit card, and I couldn't trust her with mine, so whenever she wanted to purchase a song, she'd ask me, and we'd decide how she was going to pay for it. Once that was established, I'd put my credit card info in the app and purchase the song for her. Then I'd immediately delete the credit card details.

On this particular day in the car, Beth confessed, "I don't know what's going on, but I was somehow able to buy some songs, and it let me. So, I may have bought a few songs on iTunes, Mom."

I was confused about how she could do that, and she was, too. This admission was the autism naivety coming out in her. She was rarely deceptive to me. She was usually an open book, telling me things I really didn't want to know. When I got home that day, I checked into iTunes and discovered this girl had "accidentally" charged $250 worth of songs on my credit card.

"What the heck, Beth!" I grumbled as I looked at the list of songs.

"I don't know why it was letting me do it! I thought it was a free day or something, so I just kept doing it."

I was not happy, and I let her know. But as I stewed about it, I also wondered if iTunes customer service might have compassion on this huge purchase because of Beth's disability and impulsivity. A pipe dream, right? They probably hear stories like this routinely.

I decided to call and explain the situation, and God bless them, they gave me a complete refund! They were compassionate and kind. They had a department for this type of thing. I don't know if they still make allowances for situations like this, but they sure made a fan out of me that day.

I knew Beth couldn't fill in all the information required to make an online purchase. She'd never done that before (nor since, to my knowledge). If she didn't do it, I still don't understand how my card number got into my account, unless I forgot to remove it after a previous purchase. I was much more careful about my credit card after that.

Beth was impulsive in other more dangerous ways. When she was in a bad place, we locked up our knives because she said things like, "I'm going to kill you while you're sleeping!" We didn't think we needed to worry, because of that mouthy problem she had, but we still locked up the knives. On rare occasions, when she seemed especially volatile, we locked our bedroom door.

We also locked up the medicines. This was where Beth's impulsivity was demonstrated most devastatingly. Beth had suicidal ideation throughout her teens and early twenties. She said it rarely went away. Life was so hard for her.

She was about 17 the first time she overdosed with Tylenol. She was obviously upset about something, but there wasn't an actual incident that made her grab a bottle of pills, at least not that I recall. It was an impulsive act. She had her one friend (at the time) over when it happened. This girl, Jenna, was attending the same school as Beth. Jenna is the one who told me.

I was panic-stricken at first. Greg was home, and we started asking Beth questions but tried not to increase her stress. We knew it would be really horrendous if she took off outside and started running. I called Chad, who lived nearby. He was a firefighter/paramedic by this time. He arrived quickly and sat down with Beth. He knew how to talk to her, how to deescalate the emotions. He encouraged her to go to the hospital, which she didn't want to do. We explained that a bottle of Tylenol pills could injure her liver—and may do worse. She started getting fearful at that point. Of course, she had no clue of the ramifications of what she did. It was just an impulsive act of a mentally ill brain.

I remember Chad saying, "Abby (their baby) wants to see her aunt Beth around as she's growing up. She needs you." Beth was getting quieter and quieter as this calming conversation continued. Finally, she agreed to go with me to the ER.

As I write this, I wonder why we didn't just call 911 and have an ambulance come to take her to the hospital. That may have been a better thing to do, although we would have had to do it carefully and quietly, without her knowing, or she may have run out the door before they arrived. This was our first overdose experience with Beth, and we were in shock, and didn't know how to react.

Jenna, Beth, and I took off for the ER. As soon as we arrived, which was only 10 minutes at most, Beth started throwing up by the side of the road. That was a good sign.

They gave her charcoal treatment to help her get rid of the rest of her stomach's contents and did several medical tests. Fortunately, her impulsive act did not affect her liver or anything else. I thanked God for His merciful blessing.

Jenna, Beth, and I sat in that little curtained-off area in the emergency room all night. There was little sleep happening. I was in shock, trying to face the gravity of the situation. It gave me plenty of time to think about Beth's life, from the day we picked her up at the adoption agency through all of the thousands of days leading up to this night. It made me consider how we would react if she had been successful in her overdosing plan. It made me fearful for her future and ours. It made me remember that I really should only live one day at a time. Just today. Today has enough trouble of its own. Yes, indeed.

Maralee Parker

As of this writing, she has lived through four or five overdoses. Overdosing was a reactionary decision, a spur-of-the-moment, impulsive act in each instance. It wasn't a result of thinking about it for weeks or months. It usually stemmed from something that frustrated her in the moment, although she obviously wasn't in a stable mental place when the overdoses happened. At the moment, she felt like there was no better option and life wasn't worth living, so she grabbed a bunch of pills.

Most of the time, she chose Tylenol. Once she overdosed on one of her psychiatric drugs, but fortunately, it did not have life-threatening results from an overdose.

I taught her that "suicide is a permanent solution to a temporary problem." She learned that phrase and has it embedded in her heart now. I pray she remembers it if she is ever tempted to follow through on suicidal thoughts again. I have reminded her, when she was stable, how we never know what's around the corner. Good things could be there! Wonderful, new opportunities, new friends, new pets, happiness. We just need to take life one day at a time, do the best we can, and trust God each step of the way. When things get really tough, we can look back and remember how much we have to be grateful for and realize that this is just a moment in time, just a short chapter, perhaps. Life can get better. We have to find our hope in that and look forward to a brighter future.

With each of her overdoses, she'd end up first in a regular hospital, with a hired "sitter" in her room 24/7 to watch her so she didn't try to kill herself. I would be there during the day with her or as long as the hospital would let me stay. It was awkward and annoying to have a stranger be there with us at every moment, but I understood the rationale.

When she was medically stable, she would be moved to a behavioral hospital. There she received counseling and group therapy to talk about what led her to the overdose. Sometimes she had a psychiatric medication adjustment. I had mixed feelings about that because we had worked with our psychiatrist for many years. He knew her history. He knew what we had tried and what worked and what didn't. Obviously, if she was in a behavioral hospital, her current medication cocktail was not doing a great job. I realized that, but still, I felt uneasy starting over with new meds prescribed by someone who didn't know her or her history.

Eventually, we would have a family meeting to make a plan for her release. I'm so thankful none of the overdoses resulted in damage to her liver or other organs. *Thank you, God!*

When she was hospitalized, she usually became a model patient. She acted normal—as normal as she could—and smiled and answered questions when the medical staff asked. I'm sure they wondered what the problem was since Beth didn't present as sad and depressed. If you talk with other parents who have experienced this, I think you'll hear the same story. Our kids can become Academy Award-winning actors in front of medical staff, psychiatrists, or the police, because they don't want to be there. That makes diagnosing them so much harder since a blood test can't measure psychiatric illness. How I wish it could!

Sometimes I think Beth actually liked being in a behavioral hospital. She had other people to talk to instead of living in her lonely room at home day after day. Her behavioral hospital experience was similar to a dormitory living situation, so she was behind locked doors with the others 24/7 for meals, free time, sleeping, and meetings. They started bonding. Don't get me wrong. She always wanted to come home, but I did see signs that she enjoyed being included in a group, even if it was a group no one else wanted to belong to.

One very sad night, months later, after she had been released from her hospital stay, Beth came to the side of my bed before I fell asleep (Greg was already sleeping). She was quietly crying. She explained to me, very earnestly, that sometimes she just didn't want to live anymore. She said heaven was going to be so much better than the life she had on earth, so it didn't make any sense to stay here. Then she very seriously asked me if I would help her end her life. That is something no mother should ever hear. I took a deep breath and started reassuring her of our love for her, telling her this was a difficult time, but suicide was permanent, and it was not the answer to her sadness. I listened to her talk it out, and by the time we finished, she seemed to be feeling better, and we both went to bed. I can't say I went to sleep, though. I had some praying to do first.

It's been seven years since her last hospitalization. I pray I will never again have to sit in an ER or hospital room with my daughter for psychiatric reasons.

Impulsivity came into play when she overdosed and when she ran away from home. It would be a situation where she just exploded, and all she knew to do was to run out the front door to escape (fight or flight). She was often barefoot or didn't grab a coat when it was cold out. I would jump in the car and drive the neighborhood, looking for her. If I found her, I'd follow her at a distance, giving her space until she was calmer and ready to come home (or freezing). She liked to go to the nearby school playground or to a secluded area behind a neighborhood church to think. I always looked in those places. I usually would call a girlfriend or two and ask them to pray. I love my girlfriends! Sometimes I'd call her special friend, who might come to help her calm down. Beth would much rather talk to her friend than her mother when she was angry.

As she got older, I let her go and return when she was ready, if she ran during daylight. I think she was surprised I didn't follow her. Maybe not following her helped her work through her anger more quickly or helped her realize she wasn't running from anyone. I don't know. Sometimes a parent needs to have boundaries regarding how far they will go—literally and figuratively. I just wanted her to be safe. I couldn't not search for her when it happened at night.

Sometimes when we were in a store like Walmart, Beth would walk down aisles and impulsively put things in the cart. If I knew one or two things were needed, I would buy them. But she often would start putting many things in the cart.

"We can't buy all of that," I'd tell her.

"I know, Mom. I just put it in there in case we want to buy it." Usually, she would get in these moods when she was manic or in a bad place mentally, and I would be walking on eggshells just taking her into a store. I worried that she would get angry about something or run out the door. Beth was so unpredictable. So, I sometimes let her "shop and drop" things into the cart because it seemed to improve her mood. When it was time to pay, I sometimes would go back and place the things on the appropriate shelves so the clerks wouldn't have to do it. I felt sorry for them and guilty for giving them work. But I confess, sometimes I didn't put the stuff back, and we'd leave a cart half full of items. I felt lucky if I could just get what I needed and get Beth out of the store and back into the car without a scene. I'm sorry, store clerks!

One time she had been hospitalized for an overdose and was in the hospital a week or two. On the day she was released, she drove (when she was still driving) to Jenna's house. On the way, she stopped at a store for something. While she was there, unbelievably, she shoplifted again. But this time, it was DVD sets, totaling about $200! After she was caught, she called me, and I met her there in the manager's office and tried to explain she had just been released from a mental hospital that day. I asked for compassion, but he didn't want to hear it. He was prosecuting.

That was impulsive. There was no reason for her to want to steal those DVDs. Obviously, her brain wasn't working well yet. She had changed medication at the hospital, and I feel that had something to do with that horrible, impulsive act, which led to more time in court. The court decided to let her do the Second Chance Program for a second time, but the format had changed, requiring an eight-hour day of class. There was no way she could tolerate eight straight hours of class. Ultimately, the arrest went on her record, and it's still there.

We had determined by this time that Beth would probably not be able to hold down a job, so a "record" wouldn't be as damaging for her as it might be for someone else. There was really nothing else we could do, anyway.

One afternoon I was driving home, and she was screaming at me, furious about something, as usual. We were on a beautiful country road when she grabbed her iPod and threw it out the open window as far as she could, into the swampy weeds. No logic there! With her unhinged state of mind, there was no way I was going to stop and trudge over the fence and through the muddy weeds looking for it. She would have been long gone once I stopped the car. So, she lived without an iPod for a while, even though it was one of her therapeutic calming tools.

At least it was a very old iPod. ♥

Maralee Parker

14

Angels Among Us

We believe in angels but haven't spent much time studying them. Most have heard of the famous angel, Gabriel, who appeared to Mary and Joseph to tell them about the upcoming birth of Jesus. But there are many other angel references in the Bible, too. Hebrews 1:14 is a favorite of mine: "Therefore, angels are only servants—spirits sent to care for people who will inherit salvation." I am so thankful for those "ministering spirits" that help us along life's way, whether we recognize them or not.

While they may not be angels as far as the Biblical definition goes, Beth has had a slew of angels in her life. Every time we come across a person who is so unexpected but so very helpful in our lives, I thank God for the blessing. He knows. He directs our paths and provides what is needed.

The first time this happened was with the childcare worker God provided. After Beth was a couple of months old, I needed to go back to work. It was hard to leave her, but through people I knew, God led me to Linda, a wonderful Christian mother who lived near us. She was gifted with caring for kids and had several she watched and several of her own. She was basically Beth's second mom. Beth was in her care from infancy to preschool and beyond. She spent all school days off and summers at Linda's house. Linda provided stability, security, and lots of love for Beth (and Chad!). Beth was also able to be around other kids, which was important with her autistic social challenges. What a gift we were given with Linda. She was indeed an angel.

A second angel was that collaborative interventionist when Beth transitioned from private to public school in fifth grade. Brenda and I got off to a rough start, but our relationship rerouted, we became friends, and her intervention helped Beth in fifth and sixth grades. Brenda was instrumental in helping to plan Beth's middle school IEP and came to support us in some of the stressful IEP meetings throughout that horrible seventh-grade year to help us accurately explain Beth's needs. (What an amazing turnaround from our first conversation!) Brenda was indeed an angel, and we are so grateful for her.

When Beth was in high school, I was still working full-time. I tried to think of ways to get her involved with someone who could stretch her interests outside of her TV shows, video games, and movies. I hired a young college student (who was studying psychology) to spend three hours a week with Beth, just to hang out and talk and be a good example. Kaitlyn was an amazing, kind girl. They made lemon bars together, went for walks, talked about school issues, and had fun. If they went for ice cream, Kaitlyn would encourage Beth to order and pay, so she would get more comfortable doing that. Kaitlyn would do a mini-journal for me when she turned in her hours so I could hear her thoughts about Beth's reactions to their activities. Kaitlyn even invited Beth over to her apartment to stay overnight, which Beth loved. When Beth was in the behavioral hospital for teens, Kaitlyn came to see her. She cared. She was wonderful—another angel sent from God.

When Kaitlyn moved on, a couple of others also spent time with Beth when I was working. Beth never questioned it. I think she was grateful to have someone around to do stuff with. All of those mentors (angels) were so appreciated. They fulfilled a need in Beth's life—and mine—at that time.

Alyssa is another angel in Beth's life. I mentioned earlier that Beth met Alyssa in her driver's education class. Beth could never initiate a conversation and had some trouble carrying on a conversation when someone else initiated it. But somehow, a connection happened between Beth and Alyssa. I still remember the day Alyssa called Beth after the course concluded. I was thrilled! I was so encouraged, thinking this might be a new friendship for Beth. That friendship went deep and has remained 15 years later. Alyssa is the most loving, generous person. She loves Beth and makes it a priority to be there for her.

I remember one weekend when Greg and I were at our Michigan summer home. Beth didn't want to go and was old enough to stay home alone, although that made me very nervous. Greg and I needed time away, and Beth sometimes appreciated some solitude, as well.

This particular Saturday night, I was in bed when I received a call from a panic-stricken Beth around midnight, telling me, between sobs, that she was cleaning her hamster cage when she accidentally (it's that proprioception thing again) pushed the door down as the hamster was trying to run through, and she thought she killed it! It wasn't moving. She was extremely upset and wanted someone to be with her. She had tried to call Alyssa but hadn't gotten through. She asked me to call her. After talking with Beth, I called Alyssa, and she answered! She was just leaving a Pink concert and was on her way home. I brought her up to speed and asked if there was any way she could stop at our house for a few minutes. Of course, she could!

This was just one example illustrating Alyssa's kindness to Beth. It's been repeated many times over the years. I'm so grateful for her. She's an angel!

Another angel is Beth's friend Sara who met Beth through a mutual friend, and they have stuck together for about 12 years now. Sara loves Beth and makes sacrifices to spend time with her, even though she's now a busy lady, working full-time, married, and a mom. Beth so looks forward to hanging out with Sara. I'm so thankful for Sara and that this friendship is deep, sweet and has stood the test of time.

This chapter wouldn't be complete if I didn't tell you about my amazing friend, Ruth. Another middle-of-the-night crisis occurred when Greg and I were at our summer Michigan home. The phone woke me up, and like before, Beth was sobbing so much that I couldn't understand her. My heart rate shot up.

"Beth, I can't understand you. Slow down. Take a deep breath. Tell me what's wrong."

She finally was able to get it out. "Bun-Bun is dead! I went to his cage and found him dead!"

Then I understood. Her beloved pet bunny had died unexpectedly. She'd had him for several years. Of course, it had to happen when she was home alone.

"Is there anyone you know who could come and be with me? I don't want to be alone," she sobbed.

It was 1:00 a.m. I thought about it and wondered if Alyssa could come over. "Beth, I'll call Alyssa and see if she can come over and be with you."

Unfortunately, Alyssa didn't pick up the phone.

Then I thought about Ruth. Ruth is a good friend from my church, and she has a reputation for caring about people. She is one of those people who doesn't need much sleep. I knew she often stayed up late reading, so I hesitantly called her. Unbelievably, she answered. She had been reading and had just settled down to go to sleep. I told her the story, and she said, "Sure. I can go over there." What an angel!

I called Beth and told her Ruth was on the way. She was relieved someone would be with her in her time of sorrow. As I lay down in bed, I thought, *Thank you, God, for Ruth!* I was so grateful. The next thing I remember, my phone rang. I groggily said, "Hello?"

"Everything's okay."

"Who is this?" I asked.

"It's Ruth! You know, the one who came over in the middle of the night to be with your daughter?"

I woke up, chuckled, and apologized for falling asleep, then thanked her profusely for being there for Beth. What a friend! But she wasn't done.

If you recall, we had Beth's dead hamster professionally cremated after Beth tried the DIY cremation. I knew she'd now want to get Bun-Bun cremated, too. I know my girl. If a hamster cremation costs $75, I couldn't imagine the cost of a rabbit. This was not happening.

A day or two later, when I was whining to Ruth about the dilemma, she casually said, "I can do it."

"Excuse me? What did you say?"

"I can do it." I chuckled and wondered how she was going to pull this off. Ruth is an amazing person—very generous and kind. And she is confident. She thinks she can do anything. She also loves a challenge.

Maralee Parker

She picked up Bun-Bun and took the deceased rabbit to her house. I was actually back in town but was with my 91-year-old mom, who needed emergency gallbladder surgery. I stayed in the hospital with her and at her home when she was released. Ruth and I were texting each other with updates. I told her I'd go to the dollar store and buy a little container for the ashes, but she insisted that she would get one. I left it all in her capable hands.

Then I started worrying. *What would the ashes look like? Would it look like the hamster ashes? How could Ruth possibly make the ashes look like a professional cremation? Would Beth be upset if it was different?*

I pondered these questions as I cared for my mother.

The following Sunday morning, we were sitting on the right side of the church sanctuary, our normal spot. Ruth came in and sat in her usual spot on the left side of the room. A few minutes later, I received a text from her, saying, "Bun-Bun is in the house."

It was difficult to stifle my laughter. I turned around and gave her a look. After church, she delivered "the goods" to me in a sweet little box. I snooped, and the ashes were perfect—just like the hamster ashes. When I arrived home, I gave the box to Beth, who was very happy to have her Bun-Bun with her—forever.

Ruth also accompanied Beth to one of her anime conferences when I couldn't attend. Ruth's kindnesses have blessed us many times.

One time Ruth invited a friend to attend a church gathering with her. This lady's name was Val, and by the end of the evening, I was holding Val's business card. She was an at-home seamstress. Not only was she a seamstress, but on the side, I think she was in God's angelic army. Over the next few years, Val sewed or tailored several anime costumes for Beth. She hemmed jeans and fixed other clothing. Beth's only five feet tall, so her jeans are always too long. She sewed at least half a dozen mermaid tails. Val did it all for such a reasonable price and always with a huge smile on her face. Beth and Val had a connection because Val had done some missionary work in Japan when she was single. She loves Japan, and so does Beth. There was just something there that clicked between them. Val was another angel sent from God to meet Beth's needs.

Beth battled depression often, especially after high school, when the security of a daily schedule with familiar people was missing in her life.

Sometimes she would beg, "Can we just go somewhere, anywhere, to get away for a day or two?" Sometimes she'd say, "Can we fly somewhere, Mom? I really want to go on a plane again."

Thinking of our budget, I would usually mumble, "We'll see. I'd like that, too." That would usually take care of it. She liked to dream about things, even if they weren't going to happen. She needed something to anticipate.

Then another angel named Victoria showed up. I had worked with Victoria at a local university until she moved to Florida. One day, she was back in our area and stopped at the office to surprise us. She asked, "Anybody free for lunch today?"

It turned out that one other lady and I were free, so we joined her. After lunch, she announced, "The welcome mat is always out for you to come see me in Florida. I have two beautiful guest rooms ready if you ever want to visit!" She sounded very sincere about the offer.

I remember sitting in the back seat of her car, thinking, *Wow. This sounds tempting. Is she the answer to Beth's prayer? Would this work—to go visit Victoria in Florida for a change of pace for a few days? Would she mind if I brought Beth?* I felt God's spirit nudging me to seriously consider it, even though I felt I didn't even know Victoria that well. This was absurd!

Victoria was a licensed counselor, so I knew she understood mental illness. That was another plus. When we got back to the office, I pulled her aside and briefly filled her in on my life's challenges. Again, she was more than enthusiastic about encouraging both of us to come and visit her!

That's just what we did. We made a plan and hopped on a plane. Victoria picked us up when we arrived. She had a gorgeous home and two beautiful guest rooms, just as she said. She had a lovely lanai, too. The weather was warm as contrasted with Chicago's subzero temperatures. We had hours to talk and laugh, with and without Beth. She understood much of what Greg and I were experiencing. It was so therapeutic for me, as well as Beth. We squeezed in a visit to Walt Disney World one day and the ocean another day. (This Disney visit went much better than it did when she was younger). It was an incredible getaway—just what the doctor ordered.

Our tummies were full of Victoria's top-notch cooking, and our souls were full from her wisdom, love, and friendship. It was a trip sent from God, and He used Victoria to make it happen.

Vic Mignogna is another angel in Beth's life. Vic is a talented voice actor, well known for his voice-overs for Japanese anime shows. He voiced Edward Elric in the Fullmetal Alchemist series, for any anime lovers out there.

Beth started following him years ago and attended his panels at the many anime conventions. She and I stood in line for hours at every convention to get his autograph and a hug from Vic. Teens and young adults love him. He has a fun, charismatic personality, and he treats each fan with kindness and respect.

One thing I love, other than him bringing a smile to Beth's face, is the way he naturally weaves his faith into his work. He loves Jesus and lets that be known. For example, he recorded the New Testament book of John and gave the free CDs to his fans at conventions. Sometimes he would hold an impromptu Sunday morning gathering for those who wanted to attend, where he shared his faith story.

He has definitely had an impact on Beth's faith. She emails him occasionally to ask him to pray for a sick horse or whatever the current need is, and he always responds. Who could have predicted that a voice actor at a convention for people who love Japanese anime would sail into Beth's life with spiritual encouragement? Only God. Only God!

One last angel I want to mention is Georgette. Beth doesn't own a horse anymore, but that doesn't mean she's left the horse world. She loves horses and wants to be around them for years to come, if at all possible. She even loves the smell of a horse barn (horse lovers will understand). Horses are therapeutic for her. She qualified for disability, so she gets governmental aid, but there isn't a lot of money to use for equine therapy now.

After selling Prince, she wanted to find an affordable nearby shareboard again. That is easier said than done. We would drive around our area and stop at horse barns to ask if anyone was interested in shareboarding. That was rather embarrassing for me. Beth would never talk; it always had to be me. But I put myself out there—for her. (It's unusual to drive up to a horse barn on private property and ask if anyone knows of an available shareboard situation.) Sometimes, if we found a possibility, she would even do a test ride. But nothing seemed to be clicking—until we stopped at Sunset Hill, a horse farm not far from us.

There we did find someone interested in having Beth ride her horse, as she wasn't riding much anymore. She gave a very affordable monthly price, and Beth started shareboarding again. It went well for a couple of years. She enjoyed spending time at a barn again. Unfortunately, the horse became sick and ultimately passed.

The barn owner, Georgette, was familiar with Beth's needs by this time and stepped up to offer one of her horses as a shareboard. She has been incredibly supportive and kind to Beth. Beth has found a home at Sunset and hopes to be there for many years to come. It's very close and affordable, plus Georgette and Beth have forged a sweet relationship. We are so thankful!

This chapter wouldn't be complete if I failed to acknowledge our friends, especially my girlfriends, who walked the journey with us for the past three decades. I need to mention Gayla, who has been with me since way before Beth was born, always with a listening ear and a praying heart. I had a handful of other very close friends, as well, who were always ready to listen to me vent, cry, or beg for prayers on our behalf. I wasn't one to pick up the phone (I hate talking on the phone), but my girlfriends would get emails—lots and lots of them. They'd respond with encouragement, sympathy, and the promise of prayer for us. They were my angels—again and again.

God has blessed us with many special people and situations throughout Beth's life—too many to list in this book. I keep seeing God show up in the most unusual circumstances. We realize all blessings come from Him, and we're grateful. "Whatever is good and perfect is a gift coming down to us from God our Father" (James 1:17a).

God uses people to bless others. Go be a blessing for someone today! ♥

Maralee Parker

15

I Believe in Miracles

Beth was in her mid-20s, and life continued to be routine and difficult. Greg and I had given up dreams of a serene retirement, realizing we would be responsible for Beth until we died, and we most certainly needed to make a plan for her when we were gone. Sometimes Greg and I would talk, with resignation, that this wasn't what we had signed up for when we adopted this beautiful little baby girl in 1988. Ultimately, we had put our trust in God then and now. This was the prayer Greg, Chad, and I prayed almost every night while waiting for Bethany to arrive: "Lord, please send us the special baby girl You want us to have. Help us be patient until she gets here." We trust that He answered that prayer—His way, for His purposes.

Each day, Greg and I went off to work, grateful to get away from the house and into a "normal" setting for a few hours. Greg worked long hours, partly because he tends to be a workaholic and partly because he didn't want to face the challenges at home.

While we were at work, Beth was home alone. She did a lot of sleeping, eating, watching TV and movies, and visiting the horse barn once or twice a week (with me). Occasionally she'd get together with a friend. But overall, she was still an angry kid (25 in biological age, but not developmentally). That bipolar depression always surfaced as anger for her. She could be sweet as could be—until something set her off.

It was about this time that she decided she wanted to have a boyfriend again. She had enjoyed having a boyfriend for several years in high school and beyond but hadn't dated since then. She decided to sign up on an online dating site.

How do you think I felt about that when she told me? Imagine my facial expression. My outward expression showed raised eyebrows and surprise, while my inward reaction was more along the lines of YOU HAVE GOTTA BE KIDDING ME! Here's my very naïve, attractive, 25-year-old daughter (who acts 13), who may connect online and then ride off in a car with an unknown man who has little clue about her situation. It terrified me.

Beth can look fairly normal at first meeting. Once you start talking with her, a person can detect that she may struggle with some challenges. But at first glance, which is what men would see in her online picture, her disabilities were not obvious.

It was yet another opportunity to trust God. But it was not easy. I tried to prepare her for any situation she might encounter.

She did meet one young man who seemed polite and trustworthy. When he first came to our house, he brought Beth a gift and me flowers. I liked that guy! He liked anime, too, so we invited him to join us for an anime convention after two or three dates. Greg and I decided to use it as a little family vacation since it was a few hours away in Ohio. Beth's girlfriend, Alyssa, was also going with us, so it would be a casual event, not a date for Beth and her new friend. We'd just be one big happy family. Right? What could go wrong?

All was well for a while. Then Beth decided she wanted to break up with the guy halfway through the convention. We had to travel six hours home together in our SUV after that. Can you say awkward? I love my daughter, but sometimes she makes life so challenging.

After that, she went out with another guy who told her he was prettier than she was. That was the only date with him.

Then she met someone named Rick. He was into Japanese anime, too. They chatted online for a short time, then decided to meet. When the day came, he pulled into the driveway, and I quickly took a picture of his license plate (just in case I needed it later). A mother has to do what a mother has to do.

He seemed like a nice enough guy. He was friendly and talkative with me. I must have said something about being wary of Beth doing online dating because he suddenly said he would be happy to provide his name, address, and phone number, which he did.

Maralee Parker

Hmm. That's kind of unusual. But I'll take it!

Beth and Rick went to Sushi Station for an enjoyable dinner, from what I heard later. After dinner, Rick asked, "What would you like to do now?"

"I could show you my horse," Beth suggested. Off to the horse barn they drove. Rick got an accurate view of who Beth is, and what's important to her, right from the start. I heard later he was very intimidated, never having been around horses.

"That horse is huge!" was Rick's quote I heard later from Beth.

That night signaled the beginning of a new chapter in Beth's life. More accurately, it was the beginning of a new book.

Do you believe in miracles? ♥

16

Happily Ever After

Rick quickly became a fixture in Beth's life. He liked Beth. Beth liked him. They talked on the phone and started seeing each other regularly. They were smitten.

There are two interesting stories about the early days of their relationship. First, Rick had joined the online dating service, narrowing responses to women living within 20 miles of his home. Shortly after he joined, his family moved. Prior to their move, he wasn't within 20 miles of Beth. After the move, he was. Thus, Beth showed up as a potential person for him. Rick loves to tell that story.

Second, a friend of Rick's had set him up on a blind date, to occur the day after he went out with Beth for the first time. After he and Beth hit it off so well, he called his friend early on the morning of the planned date and apologized, explaining he couldn't go. He had found someone he was very interested in and didn't feel it would be right to start anything with someone else.

When I heard that story, I just chuckled. It just seemed like it was meant to be, right from the start.

Rick and Beth moved along quickly in their relationship. They started dating in February. By March, he had given her a promise ring!

Rick has some challenges, too, and, like Beth, he's on disability with Social Security. He has a very rare physical disorder called Alport syndrome, which can affect the eyes, ears, and kidneys. Unfortunately, he had to have a kidney transplant in 2011. One amazing thing about that is he's adopted just like Beth, yet his non-biological sister matched him and was able to donate a kidney to him. That's crazy. Wonderful, awesome, crazy!

A few months later, Rick gave Beth a bigger ring and asked her to marry him. I was thankful Beth had found a nice guy, but I wasn't convinced they were going to last long term. Beth was typically very fickle. She could love something one day and want nothing to do with it the next. It was that attention span problem I was concerned about. So, I didn't know how to react, especially when Beth started saying, "We need to plan a wedding, Mom!" (Here's another great opportunity for you to imagine the look on my face when I heard that.)

Beth still struggled regularly with anger outbursts. She had days when we'd see her normal sweet and shy personality. But she also could get mad at the drop of a hat. Then her behavior would exhibit what we had always experienced—yelling, profanity, throwing things, or running out the door and off into the neighborhood. She still was not easy to be around, yet Rick saw past that. He saw her heart.

We had been seeing her psychiatrist regularly for over 18 years, since she was seven. Rick started attending our appointments with Dr. Puga, too, so he could give his input. (Beth always wanted me to attend with her. Her anxiety made it hard for her to talk.) Beth realized she had an anger problem. She didn't want to act like she did, especially now that she was in a relationship with Rick. She knew she could be difficult and didn't want him to walk out on her.

I'll never forget the appointment with Dr. Puga when he said there were only two more treatment options available. He said Beth was a complicated case and was "treatment resistant." We had tried so many medications over the years we had been working with him without much success. There was one more medication we could try. It was an old-school antipsychotic named Clozaril. However, it would require a weekly blood draw because it could have a detrimental effect on her white blood cells, which could prove fatal. After six months, she could have the blood drawn every other week. After one year, she'd need it done monthly, for as long as she remained on the medication.

The only other option, Dr. Puga explained, was ECT (electric shock therapy). Greg and I had educated ourselves and knew ECT had come a long, long way since the 1975 movie *One Flew Over the Cuckoo's Nest*. We knew of people who had it and benefited from it. It was a viable option.

Amazingly, Beth decided she would try Clozaril. This is the girl who couldn't stand needles—the girl who hid under the chair at the hospital when they tried to take blood when she was a child. She was now committing to a weekly blood draw, so her moods might improve for Rick's benefit.

I might point out that she never volunteered to do this for my benefit or her dad's benefit, but she was up for it if it would help her be more stable for Rick. Hey, I didn't care. I was just thrilled she was willing to try it.

In the spring of 2014, she started on Clozaril. It always takes a few weeks to see the results of a med change, so we didn't expect to see improvement immediately, but it wasn't long before we did see very positive changes. Beth wasn't raging anymore. She became more stable and less angry. She was happier and laughed more. Everyone was happier and laughed more!

After a few months, we rarely saw Beth's anger. Clozaril was nothing short of a miracle drug for her. We got our sweet, shy Beth back! She's been on that medication for almost seven years at the time of this writing, and it continues to work so well with her brain. It was the medication that fit her particular brain wiring. I wish she had been willing to try it years ago.

It's important to note that it doesn't mean it will work for someone else just because it worked for her. We have a friend whose daughter has similar issues, and she jumped on the Clozaril bandwagon after hearing how effective it was for Beth. It didn't do a thing for her daughter. Everyone's brain chemistry is unique and responds differently to medications. But for Beth, Clozaril was the answer.

It's also important to add that there are almost always tradeoffs when taking a psychiatric medication. A person has to measure the good things the drug does for them against any negative side effects and decide if it's worth it for them.

Clozaril causes Beth to drool when she sleeps. Her pillowcase often gets soaked. It's not fun. She's tried taking a medication to help with it but didn't feel it made much difference. So, she lives with it because Clozaril has changed her life.

Antipsychotics also often cause tremors. Beth has them. Her hands are shaky, sometimes more, sometimes less, but she lives with it because Clozaril has changed her life.

These types of meds sometimes can cause weight gain. Beth has gained 75 pounds since she first started on antipsychotics as a 15-year-old. But she lives with it and tries to fight the weight gain because Clozaril has changed her life.

So, Beth and Rick wanted to proceed with wedding planning. They had ideas. I listened politely but didn't have much to say. I wasn't sure how I should react. Weddings are expensive. I was at an impasse. I still wasn't sure this was really going to happen. Should I forge ahead and start planning with them, hoping it would take place? I didn't know what to do.

When Beth had her next therapy appointment, I snuck in before her, as I sometimes did, to provide my observations on how Beth was doing. I shared my concern with the counselor. *Do we fork out thousands of dollars as down payments for this wedding, which may or may not happen? What do I do?*

She gave me very sound, practical advice. She said, "I think Rick would have left already if he was going to go anywhere."

How wise that was! Simple but profound. I pondered it and decided she was right. Rick would have left by this time if he wasn't in for the long haul. Beth had certainly given him reason to consider leaving, with her volatile mood swings (before Clozaril). Beth also seemed very committed to Rick. I think she would have ended the relationship by this time if she wasn't sure she wanted to spend her life with this man.

Beth and Rick were spending most of their time together by this time. I knew they had been intimate (Beth has difficulty keeping secrets, remember?). Greg and I pondered it but finally decided to allow Rick to move in. He lived almost an hour away, and they were engaged now. He was driving home in the middle of the night just to want to drive back the next day. This decision is not one I'm proud of, but it was a decision made for this unique situation. I believe that sex is for marriage, for the one you will spend your life with, and for only that person. I was becoming more convinced that Rick and Beth were going to spend their lives together. There would soon be a wedding. (I better get started planning it.)

They moved into our basement. That was an interesting time. Beth and all of her animals and Rick lived in one end of the basement. We cleaned it out and tried to make it as cozy as we could. We had to get used to some of their unique quirks we didn't appreciate, like watching empty toilet paper rolls collect on the floor in the bathroom. They just couldn't seem to put a new roll on the holder and toss the old cardboard roll. It became a joke between Greg and me because we eventually realized we could not change their behavior. We tried!

We had to get used to midnight fast food runs. Why couldn't they sleep at night and get up in the morning, like normal folks? (Because they weren't normal folks.)

It wasn't fun having them live with us, but we sacrificed our privacy, comfort, and wishes so they could start their life together.

On their own, Beth and Rick had decided that they wouldn't ever have children. They didn't want to pass on their genetic challenges. We're so proud of them for making that mature decision. I know it would be incredibly difficult, if not impossible, for them to raise a child, both financially and emotionally. Babies, kids, and teenagers are challenging!

One day, Beth was complaining about the cost of birth control with their limited funds. I casually mentioned, "You know there's an easy surgery for that, so you would never have to worry about it anymore."

She looked at me incredulously as I explained. "Really? One surgery and we'd be done with birth control?" She told me to call the next day and make an appointment!

That was another answer to prayer for me. I didn't need to worry about an accidental pregnancy and all of the drama and challenge that would bring.

Although it makes me uncomfortable, I share these personal details to be helpful because I know parents reading this may be walking that path right now with their young adult kids. It's very challenging. I get it. I hope you'll find a good answer for your situation.

The time had come to plan a wedding. Beth was excited about it. She's quite the dreamer, and it seems I was the facilitator of those dreams. Of course, I also had to hold the bottom line before her at all times. It's easy to get carried away with the dream.

I still had a few qualms about it. *Would Beth be able to walk down the aisle without having a panic attack? How many people should we invite? It can't be too big, but we have a big family, and so does Rick. Will this really happen?*

We kept moving forward, one day at a time. They decided their wedding day would be February 8, 2015. We looked at four different venues, comparing the demeanor of the staff (they would have to be a bit flexible with this couple), what they offered, and the cost, of course. We decided on a nearby banquet hall that specialized in weddings. Their package included everything: food, cake, champagne, decorations, and cleanup. They showed us what the room would look like, as one was set up for another wedding that weekend. It was a beautiful presentation with chair coverings, tablecloths, and backlights. It was very fancy! We were impressed.

We were able to get the premium package that included a photo booth and dessert table and other extras for a very good price because the wedding was on a Sunday in February. That's not a busy time for them. We were blessed to benefit from that.

We put down the deposit. This was happening!

We hired a photographer, a DJ, and a florist. Beth and I went dress shopping to three or four wedding salons, and eventually, she said yes to the dress. It was a very special Mom and daughter moment. I took a picture of us to commemorate the day. (If you know me, you'd know I take pictures of just about everything.) She knew it was THE dress the minute she put it on.

Unfortunately, Beth gained weight in the months between buying the dress and the wedding day. Too many restaurant dates with Mr. Rick! So now we had a big challenge. Remember Val, that angelic seamstress? Val came to the rescue. She removed the zipper in the back and put in an adjustable corset bow closure so it would fit whether Beth lost or gained weight by February. What a lifesaver! Val has amazing skills, and we were incredibly grateful that she saved the day. She also came to the wedding, arriving early, to help Beth, if needed, with the corset back. She helped her bundle it up for the reception, too. What a sweet friend.

Beth and Rick had a lovely wedding shower from Rick's relatives at his mom's house and one from my friends at Ruth's house (the cremation expert). Beth and Rick enjoyed the fun, games, and gifts and reacted with appropriate comments and thank you's.

Rick's parents and Greg and I joined Rick and Beth in attending the pre-wedding tasting event at the banquet hall. I was still asking, *Is this really happening? Is our daughter really getting married?*

Our friend and pastor, Tim Beam, had agreed to officiate. He met with Rick and Beth for counsel privately before the wedding. They loved him, and he was very kind in meeting their special wishes for the ceremony.

I ordered anime wedding invites and matching thank you cards. They carefully chose the menu for the dinner and then were upset because they didn't have time to enjoy it at the wedding reception. They chose the Japanese cherry blossom frosting décor for their three-tiered cake.

There were a million other little details, but they were handled, one by one. The months flew by, and February 8 arrived.

It was a whirlwind day, as most wedding days are, but we have many beautiful pictures to remind us of it all. It indeed was a fairytale. Never in my wildest dreams would I have thought Beth would marry. She had been attached to my hip all of her life, but since meeting Rick, she had slowly started letting go and transferring that emotional dependence to him, as it should be.

Beth looked gorgeous! She was enjoying every minute of the excitement. She had three girlfriends in the wedding party. Alyssa was her maid of honor, tending to her every need, as usual. Sara and Liz added their love and support as bridesmaids. Celebration was in the air!

Beth had a bottle of Xanax in the cupboard for months for very stressful situations or if she felt she was having a panic attack. She very rarely used it. She took some with her for the wedding, but she didn't take one pill. I was so very proud of her determination to do this day on her own—no extra meds required.

The wedding hour had arrived. The mothers were seated. Soon Beth was escorted down the makeshift aisle by her dad, who was talking to her with every step to distract her and ease her fear. She looked stunning. Rick was eagerly waiting for her, locking his eyes on hers and memorializing the moment forever. The ceremony was brief but beautiful. I tried to stay present and enjoy every second, but I found myself slipping back, remembering many moments of her life. I'm sure all parents probably do that as their child marries. It was an incredible, surreal experience for me.

The reception followed with good food, about 100 family and friends, and fun times. Two of Beth's high school teachers were there, which meant so much to her. Beth's psychiatrist, Dr. Puga, also attended with his wife. How special! He had supported Beth and us through it all, from summersaults off his chair at age seven to surviving multiple overdoses and hospitalizations, along with talking through all of the other challenging behaviors that resulted from a sick brain. He had the joy of watching her blossom under the medication that finally helped her brain function well. We were so blessed to have him join us at the wedding celebration!

What an incredible day—a day I believed would never come. As we raised this girl and endured years and years of mental illness and the challenges it brought, we never dreamed we'd be walking Beth down the aisle to her husband one day and celebrating her marriage.

This day was totally unexpected but awesome! There were a few other very special guests in attendance that day, as well.

Beth was in her mid-teens when she began saying she wanted to meet her birth mom someday. She and I had talked about her birth mom throughout Beth's life. I didn't want her adoption to be a big secret, so we started using the word *adoption* before Beth started talking. I had several children's books about adoption that we read regularly. She grew up knowing she was adopted. It didn't seem to be a big deal one way or the other to her—just as I had hoped.

When Beth was five years old, I documented a conversation between us. Bethany saw a book about sharks at the babysitter's house. It must have had scary pictures, because all of a sudden, she was afraid of sharks. She was in the bathtub and said, "I'm thinking about those sharks again, and I'm afraid!"

"Try to stop thinking about them. Think about other things. Think about Valentine's Day that's coming soon, or Easter."

She responded, "No, I'm going to think about my mother."

I was surprised by that response and said, "Okay, think about me. Whatever you want to think about is just fine."

She replied, "No, I don't mean you; I mean my first mother. Because I love her. And I love you, too. I love both of you."

Wow. That made me happy.

She didn't have typical adoption issues, even in her teens. I never detected she felt abandoned or unloved. The adoption agency had delivered a letter from her birth mother when Beth was born and a second one a few months later. Since it was a closed adoption, those two letters would conclude the communication. When Beth was a teen, I showed her the letters. Her birth mom expressed great love for her and explained what a difficult decision it had been to move forward with the adoption plan. I believe that by seeing those words in her birth mom's handwriting, Beth realized she was loved, not abandoned, so she didn't struggle with typical adoption challenges.

She told me she would like to meet her birth mom someday.

"I'm happy to help you search for her after you're 18 and out of high school," I promised. I meant it. I didn't fear her loving her birth mom more than me or anything like that. I felt very confident that Beth loved me, even though she screamed at me a lot in her B.C. (before Clozaril) days. I could understand why she would want to meet the woman who gave her life. I could understand wanting to look at someone who may resemble you when that has never happened in your lifetime. I also knew that sometimes these situations don't turn out well. Perhaps the birth mother didn't want to be found. There is a fair amount of risk involved when someone goes searching for a birth parent.

Illinois had just begun a new program so adoptees could register their name, date of birth, and place of birth. When they became 18, they would be sent a copy of their original birth certificate (unless the birth parents had contacted the state and asked that it not happen). I helped Beth register, and after she turned 18, we received a letter with a copy of her original birth certificate, giving her mother's name.

I remember the day we received it. We were both excited! Now we had to put our detective hats on. We had to figure out how to find this person listed on the birth certificate. We Googled her right away. I don't think we discovered anything there. So, what's next? Facebook, of course. We searched Facebook and found someone with that name! As we clicked on the person's profile and photos, I knew immediately that it was Beth's birth mom. Beth looked just like her. She lived 30 minutes from us.

The agency had given us one small photocopied picture of the birth mom, along with the original letter written to Beth. That's all we had, but it did give us an idea of what she had looked like 18 years earlier. Our tattered photocopy reinforced our discovery. This was Beth's birth mom.

It was becoming real now.

I sat with Beth, asking how she was feeling. We discussed (I talked and she listened) how we should contact her because this would be a shock to her birth mom. She didn't know we were looking. She may not be aware of the state's new program for adoptees. I explained that we needed to be discreet in how we messaged her and choose our words wisely. By then, it was late, so I suggested we sleep on it and pick it up in the morning.

When I awoke the next morning, Beth was still sleeping. My computer was open to the birth mom's profile page. It quickly became clear that Beth had friended her birth mom while I was asleep, and messages were sent back and forth! So much for the careful plan.

Beth had friended her but never explained or said, "I think I'm your daughter."

So, the birth mom was saying, "I had a baby girl on October 27 of that year. Could that be you?"

After Beth got out of bed, Beth and her birth mom texted back and forth, and I jumped in, too, to help clarify things if needed. We had found her!

In the next few days, I gave the birth mom, whose name is Jeannie, the history of Beth's life as briefly as I could. I sent many adorable baby and childhood pictures to her, imagining how she might be feeling as she saw them.

I told her about our struggles and that Beth was diagnosed with bipolar syndrome, and she shared that she also had it. She wasn't sure where the autistic part came from, though.

Like Beth, Jeannie also has anxiety, so she was afraid of talking to Beth on the phone for a few days. One of her other daughters, Kara (four years younger than Beth), helped coach her through her fear. I remember the first time Jeannie and Kara called Beth. It was exciting for all of them. We arranged a meeting near their house a few days later, which was just 30 minutes away. It was a wonderful time to hug, talk, catch up, and gaze at each other. Beth had never seen anyone who looked like her. I can imagine seeing biological family with resemblance is wonderful for adoptees.

That day Beth met her birth mom, sister Kara, and Jeannie's youngest daughter, Justice (14 years younger than Beth). At a family gathering, Beth recently met her half-brother (two years younger), who was also placed via adoption. Jeannie was able to be with all four of her kids at once, something she never dreamed would happen.

Another fun story about the adoption involves the name Jeannie gave Beth at birth. She named her Susan Lee, and my name is Maralee Susan. Her given name is incorporated in mine. Beth and I have always smiled at that. It's another sign it was meant to be.

Beth visited Jeannie and her sisters occasionally over the next few years. She has invited her youngest sister to our lake house in Michigan several times. It's been a wonderful reunion for Beth, Jeannie, and the family. So, of course, we invited them to the wedding!

They were all there, all dressed up and so happy for Beth. The wedding photographer took a picture that day, as we requested, of Jeannie and her three daughters (the brother hadn't been found yet). Another special picture was taken of Beth, her birth mom, and me. Beth was happy her birth family could attend, and so was I.

After the wedding, Jeannie wrote a Facebook post under one of Beth's wedding pics, publicly thanking us for inviting her to the wedding. Not in her wildest dreams did she think she would ever be able to attend her firstborn's wedding. She was very grateful.

It was a fairytale wedding, in more ways than one. Now Beth and Rick are living happily ever after—so far! ♥

17

One Day at a Time

If you're a parent in the trenches of raising a special needs child, I wrote this book to encourage you. I want you to know that you are not alone. You may be walking a very difficult path right now with your loved one, but I'm here to testify that you don't know what's around the corner. You may have some unexpected, amazing surprises coming, as we did. I won't stick my head in the sand and promise that all mental illness struggles have a happy ending. We know that's not true. Statistics clearly inform us of suicides, suicide attempts, homelessness, and broken families that sometime result from severe mental illness. It's not easy for our ill loved ones to live their lives, and it's not easy for those of us who love them, either.

That's why we focus on living just one day at a time, doing the best we can each day. It doesn't make sense to worry about next week, next month, or farther down the road. Focus on today. Each day has enough trouble of its own. Worrying accomplishes nothing except creating stress, and perhaps, a shorter lifespan.

Just do the best you can for today, dear one. Take encouragement from our story, which has such a happy ending, although we know it's not really the end. We're in a calm phase right now, and we're enjoying it so much. We realize Beth could become immune to her medication, and then we'd be back to the drawing board again to find a different med that works with her brain. (I recently read that just because a med didn't work at one time doesn't mean it may not work years later. That is encouraging.)

Maralee Parker

Rick and Beth will soon be celebrating their seventh wedding anniversary. They not only made it to and through the wedding but have been married for years already. This is a miracle.

There's more.

There's still one more piece to this fairytale story.

My sweet mother and father bought their first home when my dad was 60 years old. They were tenant farmers most of their lives and rented a house after that. My dad didn't think the bank would give him a loan at his age, but he was wrong. Mom was eight years younger. Perhaps that came into play with the bank's decision. They got their loan and bought a tiny four-room house in 1975. I lived there with them for a year before I married Greg. They loved their house and were very proud of it. Dad passed away in 1993, and Mom lived there alone for 22 years after that. All told, that house served them for 40 years.

Fast forward to 2015. Mom was happy and proud to attend her granddaughter's wedding in February. In March, she fell in her house, needed hospitalization, and then was transferred to a rehabilitation center. She was evaluated, and we were told she should no longer live alone. That was a sad and hectic time researching appropriate nursing homes and getting her settled.

Meanwhile, her beloved little house sat empty.

In my mind, I had secretly wondered, years earlier, if Beth might be able to live there one day. It was very small, so not a lot to take care of. It was Grandma's house, so there was an emotional attachment already, which might help with the transition from our house to that house. Beth always struggled with transitions. I threw the idea out to Greg. We kicked it around, discussed it, and prayed about it.

I didn't know if Beth and Rick could live independently. Remember, they were living in our basement. Moving to Grandma's house would mean much greater independence for them (and us), although we wouldn't be far away if they legitimately needed us. Rick's parents weren't far in the opposite direction. Living in the house would mean they would need to be responsible for snow shoveling, lawn mowing, cleaning, cooking, and laundry. We decided we wouldn't know if it would work if we didn't try. We approached this with the same attitude as we had so many other things in Beth's life. We just had to try and see if we could get traction.

Greg and I decided to go for it. We talked to Beth and Rick about it to see if they wanted to do this. They were excited but also apprehensive. Rick was particularly anxious about the financial aspect. I put their income on paper and created a simple budget. I explained how it would need to work (I explained it again and again). In the end, they agreed it would be possible and were willing to do their part to make it happen. So we moved forward.

Mom bequeathed the house to my two brothers and I in equal parts, so Greg and I would need to buy out my brothers. Before we bought them out, I asked my big brothers if they would please give Beth and Rick a few months to try it out to be sure it indeed would be doable. Of course, they agreed. (They love their little sister and their niece, too.)

Beth and Rick's moving day came in April of that same year, two months after their wedding. (The timing was amazing.) Beth's first few days of living in their new home were bumpy. Remember, she had never lived away from home and me, in particular. She was very emotionally attached to me, even though she acted like she hated me for so many years.

"I don't know if we can do this, Mom," she stammered.

I think they felt a little abandoned at first. No parents lived with them to support them and help them feel safe. It was just them, morning, noon, and night. I kept calmly encouraging them to do their best and give it time—one day at a time. I told them what a wonderful opportunity this was for them now and for the rest of their lives. (I would occasionally remind Beth that her dad and I would not live forever, but she never wanted to think about that.)

Another miracle happened. One day led to another, and another. One week led to another, and another. They began to like having a place to call their own. They began to like the self-confidence growing in them as they started to manage their own lives in a more mature, independent way.

We bought the house.

Maralee Parker

They have lived there for almost seven years. They have a home, and we have a home. As I type those words, I lift my hands in praise to my God! It truly is a miracle. Greg and I have our home entirely to ourselves, something we haven't had for 40 years since Chad was born. We are loving it and are so very grateful. Greg recently retired, and because of that and the worldwide COVID-19 pandemic, we've been home together a lot—a lot, a lot. We love it! I've said it seems like we're on a second honeymoon after 45 years of marriage. We're happy together, and every day seems like Saturday.

We thank God for all of these blessings. We lift our voices in praise and gratitude to Him, from whom all blessings flow. He has blessed Beth and Rick, and He has greatly blessed us.

Another Bible verse that resonates with me is Psalms 30:5b: "Weeping may last through the night, but joy comes with the morning." That has been so true with our story. There was a great deal of weeping, frustration, exhaustion, and desperation throughout all of those years, and so much prayer, but look at us now. We do have joy—our joy came "with the morning."

Another favorite Bible verse is Lamentations 3:22–23: "The faithful love of the Lord never ends! His mercies never cease, Great is his faithfulness; his mercies begin afresh each morning." That's a verse I think of often in the morning as I sit in the quietness and thank God for His mercy and faithfulness. "Great Is Thy Faithfulness" is one of my very favorite hymns.

This book shares many stories but only touches the surface of the many experiences we had as a family throughout the past 34 years. Surprisingly, I remember many of the stories, though my memory is not the best. I am the one who buys gifts and can't find them when Christmas comes or sends the same birthday card, because "it's perfect for them," not remembering I already sent it the year before, because it was "perfect for them."

Bonus confession: I am not going into all the details, but I did buy not one, not two, but three identical red shirts for Chad one Christmas when he was 13. I proudly acknowledge that I not only bought them, but wrapped them. That was a very funny Christmas morning. The story lives on almost 30 years later.

All of that to say, my memory stinks. But I thank God for my bad memory. I consider it a gift. I thank Him because I don't remember all of the details of the heartache, the tears, the exhausting days and nights, the walking on eggshells, the advocacy I had to provide between Beth and Greg, between Beth and her friends, and between Beth and her school. I remember some of it. I remember specific stories. But overall, it's kind of a blur. It's interesting because Beth says the same thing.

That, my friends, is a huge blessing. I'm thankful.

Over the years, Greg and I would occasionally ask God, "Why? Why us?" We didn't want to accept a baby with special needs when the social worker asked us about it. We didn't feel we were cut out for it. We were career people. We just wanted a baby that would fit in, be happy, and grow up without a lot of fuss. (I'm saying this tongue-in-cheek, in case you're missing my sarcasm.)

We didn't receive an immediate answer when we asked God why He sent Beth to us, but we had some ideas. For one thing, we realized God changed us through Beth. We are not the same people we were in 1988. We are more compassionate and less judgmental. We are more patient, flexible, and less controlling. We trust God more.

God has opened our eyes to the needs of others, not just our own. Scripture says in James 1:27 that God has great love for orphans and widows, and Beth was an orphan. We came to realize we were pleasing and obeying God by loving her.

Then a new door opened in our lives because of Beth.

I researched ADHD, ODD, autism, and bipolar disorder during the challenging years. I read many books and articles and belonged to several online support groups. I heard, several times, about a national organization called NAMI, which offered a course called "Family-to-Family." I heard rave reviews about the course from people who had attended it.

When I heard it was going to be held in my town, I knew I wanted to attend.

"It's supposed to be an excellent course, Greg. Will you go with me?"

"I don't know," he said. His lack of enthusiasm was underwhelming.

I gave him time to think about it. He doesn't make quick decisions. The class didn't start for a couple of months, so I had some time. But

Maralee Parker

later, as I saw the registration deadline approaching, I asked, "That course is starting soon, and I have to register. I heard it's a really great course, and I'm planning to attend, but I'd really like you to come, too. Will you?"

He didn't respond. Then after a few seconds, he said, "I suppose."

Win! I didn't care about his lack of enthusiasm. I had agreement. I registered us, and soon we attended the first class. There were 22 of us. It was an eye-opener. We each received a binder with a pack of printed information (we received more information each week). The facilitators did a great job, leading us through a great amount of helpful information. There was time for questions and participation as well.

By the end of the first session, Greg was hooked. Both he and I looked forward to each weekly class. We learned so much, and we didn't feel alone anymore. These families were experiencing similar challenges to ours in their lives with a mentally ill loved one. We felt supported and not alone. They spoke our language. We had found our tribe.

We graduated from that NAMI course and soon began attending the monthly support group. People with an ill loved one could attend to vent, ask questions, or just feel like they weren't alone on their journey.

We liked this NAMI organization so much that we joined the board of directors for our local affiliate. When our president asked if anyone might be interested in being trained to teach the "Family-to-Family" course, we signed up. We spent a three-day weekend in Chicago, receiving training during the day in a lovely hotel and enjoying Chicago and the hotel in the evenings on our own dime. It was a lovely, memorable weekend.

We've taught the course several times now. It's rewarding to educate and encourage family members who are confused, exhausted, and have nowhere to turn. Many are in crisis over a recent mental illness diagnosis in their child or loved one. Mental illness can come on suddenly anytime. We see it often in young adults between ages 18 and 25. Parents are shocked because they feel they have suddenly lost the child they had known. It's heartbreaking.

We also agreed to lead a monthly support group for people with mentally ill family members or friends. We found the group helpful when we were in the midst of our challenges with Beth. Now we're paying it forward, trying to help others who are holding on by a thread, as well as those who have lived with a family member with mental illness for years. NAMI Family Support group is a good place to be reminded you're not alone and that others will understand your story.

As we were teaching the Family-to-Family course, I came up with a word that describes family and friends on the "outside"—those who really don't understand mental illness or the unbelievable, challenging situations we find ourselves in. I call them "civilians." They aren't part of the "inside track." They don't know the unwritten rules, the expectations, or the lack of them, or the secrets families keep. They don't know how we prepare in special ways to help our loved ones function in the outside world. They don't get it because they are not part of it. They are indeed "civilians." When we talk about this in the Family-to-Family course, most participants nod their heads. They get it. They've experienced it.

In years past, Greg and I wondered why God didn't give us a second biological baby, which was the desire of our hearts. We wondered why He led us to adoption and why He sent Beth—just the right baby.

We think a big part of the reason is NAMI. There is no way we would have been involved in this organization if it weren't for Beth. We sought it out because we needed it. Now God is using us to help other people through it. He's taught us that many hurting people in the world need love, acceptance, and support. Scripture makes it clear that Jesus had a very special place in His heart for the downtrodden, the less fortunate, the sick, or people everyone else ignored or didn't want to associate with. He wants us to show love to hurting people. We're trying to do that.

When I met Greg decades ago, he was working as an RN. His clinical rotation included time in a mental health center. He used to say that he learned a lot from that experience. He learned that he "would never work in psych!" He didn't like the grayness of it all—outcomes couldn't be measured. It wasn't a black and white science. When a doctor or nurse helps fix a heart, a gallbladder, or resets a bone, the results of their work can be seen fairly quickly. That's not true with mental illness.

You know what I have to say about that? "Never say never!" He chuckles now as he tells that story. Life is full of unexpected twists and turns.

Today, Beth is happy. She's not suicidal anymore. Her faith in God is strong. She finds it very difficult to attend a church service, but she talks to God and trusts Him. She enjoys Christian music. She sometimes will post something on Facebook about faith, and that makes my heart so happy.

This is the letter she wrote me last Christmas:

Mom,

You are everything to me. I can't imagine life without you. You do so much for Rick and I, from the simple stuff to the tougher stuff. You're there to calm me down during hard times. You also put me in my place when I need it. LOL

I wish I had the money to buy you a gift but this is the best I can do.

I love you Mom!

Merry Christmas!

Our relationship has turned 180 degrees from where it was in her angry days. She and I have mother and daughter days often where we do lunch, see a movie, or go shopping. Sometimes, it's all three! I hear from her daily on the phone. She's my girl. I love her so much.

I've heard the saying, "We plan, and God laughs." I think there's some truth in that. It's good to have goals and dreams in life. It's good to plan for the future, as long as our plan is flexible. Ultimately, it's wise to take life one day at a time, just as I've told Beth all of her life. One day at a time. Each day has enough trouble of its own.

Life rarely goes as planned. When the unexpected hits you, take it a day at a time and trust God. His mercies are new every morning, and He is so faithful.

Of that, I am sure. ♥

A Note from Beth

Life isn't easy!

You have to rely on those around you to help you through, whether it be a loving text from your best friend, cuddling with a pet, or having a fun movie night with your husband.

I still suffer from anxiety, depression, and irritability. But I have found ways to cope and get through those bad days.

I have found joy in my family, friends, pets, horses, and anime.

I have learned that you can't be reckless with the life God gave you. You are here for a reason. God has blessed me in so many ways. I'm glad He didn't give up on me.

Remember that God and people love you and care for you. Don't take them for granted. I hope this book will be a light in the dark. ♥

Beth Nicpon

Acknowledgments

I've loved writing since I was ten years old and had my first diary. Now I feel at home sitting in front of a computer, fingers flying over the keyboard. Those years of Typing I and Typing II have come in handy.

This book about raising our daughter has been a dream of mine for over 20 years. A cancer diagnosis put it on the back burner. Then I had no emotional energy to write while we were in the midst of it all with our daughter. Nor did I have an encouraging ending—until now.

I have many to thank for helping me get it finished. I want to thank people in my life who encouraged my writing: Betty Free Swanberg, my supervisor at David C. Cook Publishing. She took a chance on me, hiring me as an editor, then encouraging and mentoring me as I learned the ropes. Linda Washington, a co-worker at Cook, has also always been very encouraging, helping me believe that I have a writing voice.

Sue Reck and Cathy Davis Pezdirtz, also from D. C. Cook, both read the early manuscript and gave me helpful comments and encouragement. It was appreciated.

Thanks to Kristin and staff at Little Creek Press for their professionalism and assistance in getting the manuscript published.

I want to thank my endorsers. Thank you for taking the time to read and comment on the book. It is so appreciated!

Thanks to all the mental health professionals, especially Dr. William Puga, who have worked with our family for many years. You do good work—you've made such a difference in all our lives.

What would we do without our NAMI family? A big thanks to NAMI, Kane County North, for your commitment to serving individuals with mental health challenges and their families. Thank you for loving us and walking the journey with us.

Huge thanks to my family, especially Beth, for letting me tell the story, warts and all. I love you and am so grateful for your support. Let's pray God will use it to help others.

Finally, I'm so grateful to my God for giving Greg and me strength, one day at a time, to endure the hard years. I thank Him for answering our prayers, in His way, in His time. Psalms 50:15 says, "Trust me in your times of trouble, and I will rescue you, and you will give me glory."

Today, I'm giving God all the glory. ♥

About the Author

Maralee Brown Parker has enjoyed writing since she began keeping diaries in fifth grade.

She's a wife to Greg, mom to Chad and Beth, and grandma to Abby, Lexi, and Ethan. Her 35-year work career included time at David C Cook as an editor of Sunday school curriculum and at Judson University as marketing and enrollment manager for the Division of Continuing Education. She's a graduate of Moody Bible Institute and Judson University. She's the published author of two children's books and hundreds of devotionals for adults.

She's now happily retired, enjoying coffee every morning in the sunroom, watching the birds with her husband and two dachshunds, and thanking God for His faithfulness.

♥

Contact Me

Contact me at unexpectedmemoir@gmail.com. I'd love to hear from you.

♥

Reviews Welcomed

My goal is to have many people read this book and be encouraged. I would be honored and thankful if you'd take a moment to review it on amazon.com, barnesandnoble.com, christianbook.com, or anywhere you can find it online. Reviews and ratings influence others. Thank you!

Discussion Questions for Book Clubs

1. Tell about a time when something unexpected happened in your life. How did you react?

2. What does it say about us when we fall apart when something happens that we're not expecting?

3. Is God surprised when we face crisis? Why do you feel that way?

4. Do you feel counseling and medications are helpful tools for mental illness? Why or why not?

5. What is one thing that your challenging situation has taught you?

6. What are some ways that you've learned to cope and renew your strength as you walk through difficult days?

7. Encouragement is so needed and appreciated, for ourselves and others. What can you do to surprise and encourage your special needs loved one?

8. Take a moment to think about the "angels" in your life who have helped you and your loved one along the way. Sometimes we don't stop and thank God for these people who have come alongside us, in big or small ways. Do it now, then share a name or two with the group and what they mean to you. Perhaps you might take time to drop a note to the person to express your gratitude.

The following poem has been meaningful to many who have had broken expectations in life. I hope you enjoy it. It's my hope that you'll enjoy your trip, once you change your expectations.

Welcome to Holland

By Emily Perl Kingsley

I am often asked to describe the experience of raising a child with a disability—to try to help people who have not shared that unique experience to understand it, to imagine how it would feel. It's like this....

When you're going to have a baby, it's like planning a fabulous vacation trip—to Italy. You buy a bunch of guide books and make your wonderful plans. The Coliseum. The Michelangelo David. The gondolas in Venice. You may learn some handy phrases in Italian. It's all very exciting.

After months of eager anticipation, the day finally arrives. You pack your bags and off you go. Several hours later, the plane lands. The flight attendant comes in and says, "Welcome to Holland."

"Holland?!?" you say. "What do you mean Holland?? I signed up for Italy! I'm supposed to be in Italy. All my life I've dreamed of going to Italy."

But there's been a change in the flight plan. They've landed in Holland and there you must stay.

The important thing is that they haven't taken you to a horrible, disgusting, filthy place, full of pestilence, famine and disease. It's just a different place.

So you must go out and buy new guide books. And you must learn a whole new language. And you will meet a whole new group of people you would never have met.

It's just a different place. It's slower-paced that Italy, less flashy than Italy. But after you've been there for a while and you catch your breath, you look around ... and you begin to notice that Holland has windmills ... and Holland has tulips. Holland even has Rembrandts.

Maralee Parker

But everyone you know is busy coming and going from Italy … and they're all bragging about what a wonderful time they had there. And for the rest of your life, you will say "Yes, that's where I was supposed to go. That's what I had planned."

And the pain of that will never, ever, ever, ever go away … because the loss of that dream is a very, very significant loss.

But … if you spend your life mourning the fact that you didn't get to Italy, you may never be free to enjoy the very special, the very lovely things … about Holland.

Mental Health Online Resources

www.Nami.org

www.theMighty.com

www.nimh.nih.gov

www.samhsa.gov/

www.mentalhealthfirstaid.org

www.autismsociety.org

www.autismspeaks.org

www.mentalhealth.gov/

www.mhanational.org/

www.healthyplace.com

www.dbsalliance.org/

The End

CPSIA information can be obtained
at www.ICGtesting.com
Printed in the USA
BVHW032342030622
638835BV00006B/16